Discovering your future Through Dynamic Dialogue

(conversations)

Foreword by **Leonard Sweet**

Dave Fleming

Flagship church resources

from Group Publishing

Innovations From Leading Churches

Flagship Church Resources are your shortcut to innovative and effective leadership ideas. You'll find ideas for every area of church leadership, including pastoral ministry, adult ministry, youth ministry, and children's ministry.

Flagship Church Resources are created by the leaders of thriving, dynamic, and trend-setting churches around the country. These nationally recognized teaching churches host regional leadership conferences and are respected by other pastors and church leaders because their approaches to ministry are so effective. These flagship church resources reveal the proven ideas, programs, and principles that these churches have put into practice.

Flagship Church Resources currently available:

- *60 Simple Secrets Every Pastor Should Know*
- *The Perfectly Imperfect Church: Redefining the "Ideal Church"*
- *The Visual Edge: Compelling Video Connectors for Your Worship Experience*
- *Mission-Driven Worship: Helping Your Changing Church Celebrate God*
- *An Unstoppable Force: Daring to Become the Church God Had in Mind*
- *A Follower's Life: 12 Group Studies on What It Means to Walk With Jesus*
- *Keeping Your Head Above Water: Refreshing Insights for Church Leadership*
- *Seeing Beyond Church Walls: Action Plans for Touching Your Community*
- *unLearning Church: Just When You Thought You Had Leadership All Figured Out!*
- *Morph!: The Texture of Leadership for Tomorrow's Church*
- *The Quest for Christ: Discipling Today's Young Adults*
- *LeadingIdeas: To-the-Point Training for Christian Leaders*
- *Igniting Passion in Your Church: Becoming Intimate With Christ*
- *What Really Matters: 30 Devotions for Church Leadership Teams*
- *Discovering Your Church's Future Through Dynamic Dialogue*
- *Simply Strategic Stuff: Help for Leaders Drowning in the Details of Running a Church*
- *Preach It!*

With more to follow!

Discovering *Your Church's Future*
Through
Dynamic
Dialogue

by Dave Fleming

Flagship church resources
from Group Publishing

Discovering Your Church's Future Through

Dynamic
Dialogue

Visit our Web site: **www.grouppublishing.com**

Credits
Creative Development Editor: Paul Woods
Chief Creative Officer: Joani Schultz
Editor: Candace McMahan
Copy Editor: Ann M. Diaz
Art Director: Randy Kady
Print Production Artist: Dawn Putney, Toolbox Creative
Cover Art Director/Designer: Jeff A. Storm
Cover Illustrator: Todd Davidson
Production Manager: Peggy Naylor

Library of Congress Cataloging-in-Publication Data
Fleming, Dave, 1964-
  Discovering your church's future through dynamic dialogue / by Dave Fleming.
      p. cm.
  ISBN 0-7644-2639-7 (pbk. : alk. paper)
  1. Church management. 2. Dialogue--Religious aspects--Christianity.
3. Communication--Religious aspects--Christianity. I. Title.
  BV652.9.F58 2003
  253--dc22   2003017795

10 9 8 7 6 5 4 3 2 1   13 12 11 10 09 08 07 06 05 04
Printed in the United States of America.

{ TABLE OF Contents }

ACKNOWLEDGMENTS

FIRST, I THANK MY FAMILY, who not only allows me to write, but encourages me to do so. Thanks to my wife, Kelly, for her support and love throughout this project and many others. And thanks to my parents, who taught me how to dialogue.

To the community at North Way, I am grateful. To my colleagues and friends at North Way who are courageous enough to enter the conversation, I want you to know it's an honor to serve with you.

To all the people at Group, I could not have done this without you. Thanks to Paul Allen and Paul Woods, who believed in this project and in me. Thanks to Candace McMahan. Your editorial insight and desire to keep me headed down the right path were invaluable.

Finally, thanks to Len Sweet and Brian McLaren for their encouragement and help on this book.

by LEONARD SWEET

IT WAS HARVEST FESTIVAL TIME IN GREEN LAKE, Wisconsin, and I had been asked by the local council of churches to speak at the festival.

After the morning worship, American Baptist Pastor Karina Gygax Rodriguez and I took a fantasy stroll through the exhibit of classic cars, all shined up to look as if they had just come off the original showroom floor. I stopped to drool over an early "retractable" red Ford. When Karina asked the owner, "Did you drive it here or trailer it in?" he responded with a flare of indignation: "This is no trailer queen. I drove her here."

How many of our churches are "trailer queens"—meant not for the road, but only for show? No scratches, no dents, no flying stones to scrape the chrome. No risk to the carpet from rough gravel roads or ribbons of asphalt.

Do you think I'm exaggerating our penchant for spiritual showboating? As soon as you start getting your church "on the road again," you can count on at least one inevitability. You will hear the "key" question: "Can we trust these people with a key to the church?" Roughly translated it means: "What will happen to the carpet?"

At a conference on postmodern ministry in Winnipeg, Canada, the host pastor invited us to conclude our coffee break and reconvene in the sanctuary. In words that revealed to me my own "trailer queenism," he said, "Feel free to bring your coffee with you when you come. You can add your stain to all the others." Most of us in the church are more like the fastidious Nat King Cole, who, once he put on his trousers in the dressing room before his TV show, wouldn't sit down again until he was on the set so that he wouldn't break the crease. Our pastures of faith are maintained, while the purposes of faith have disintegrated. To fight about doctrines such as predestination without having a destination is the essence of trailer queenism.

Dave Fleming has written this book to give the church a new road-worthiness. There is an old joke from the '60s: Did you hear about the hippy who didn't know LSD from LDS? He went on a mission instead of a trip. Fleming challenges the church to trade in its tourist mind-set for a missional seriousness and sensibility. But he backs up his challenge by offering more than filled-in potholes and resurfaced cracks. He paves a new road for the church to take into the future, a road of conversation and dialogue in which dialogue is more than an exchange of ideas. As Pope John Paul II defines it, true dialogue is always "an exchange of gifts."

It almost sounds too easy. The road to the future is one of conversation and dialogue? That's it? Fleming does not pretend that there won't be detours and pitfalls on this path of dialogue. But he does insist that dialogue is the path that can take us into the future if we will "pray and not give up" (Luke 18:1).

A security officer at Los Angeles International Airport helped me understand what Jesus meant when he instructed us to "pray and not give up." My flight had brought me into LAX Terminal 6, but my connection was out of Terminal 3. Bolting from the plane, I followed the exit signs until I reached the last agent inside the secured area.

"My connection is out of Terminal 3, and I have only a few minutes to make it. Any tips you can give me?"

She straightened up, smiled, and said, "Walk it. Don't take the shuttle. Just keep going, and don't let anything stop you."

"What do you mean 'keep going?' " I shot back, looking for more specificity. "What turns will I need to take?"

"When you get outside, keep to the left of the flying saucer," she stated, even more insistent than before. "Don't let anything stop you. And pray."

Sure enough, when I got outside, the famous LAX flying saucer was in front of me. To take the shuttle to Terminal 3 would surely take too much time. But to walk to the terminal, which was hidden behind a maze of buildings, barriers, and parking garages, seemed futile and foolish. But the agent's smile and closing admonition—"and pray"— gave me the courage I needed to risk it.

Even though her words "Keep going, and don't let anything stop you" didn't seem enough, they were enough. Whenever I came to a fence, I didn't let it stop me. I went around it or climbed over it. Whenever I came to a dead end, I looked for a way around the barrier and didn't let it stop me. As I negotiated every blockade, I thought to myself, "If I had known about all these hurdles and all I would have to overcome, I wouldn't have done this." But I followed her advice, didn't let anything stop me, and sure enough, in a few minutes, there was Terminal 3.

All the roads to the future are filled with unknowns and uncertainties. But Dave Fleming has shown the church the best road to take, if only we will "pray and not give up."

Leonard Sweet
Drew Theological School, Madison, New Jersey
George Fox University, Portland, Oregon
www.preachingplus.com

MY DOG, SNUGGLES, COMMUNICATES VERY EFFECTIVELY. When she's out of water, she paws relentlessly at her water bowl and whines as if she hasn't had a drink in a week. When she needs to go outside, she scratches the door as if to say, "Is anyone listening? This is getting serious!" She can communicate what appears to be happiness and has an uncanny way of "lying low" when she's done something wrong. No doubt about it: Snuggles can communicate.

There is also no doubt that I've never once had a creative conversation with Snuggles—one that would lead to new vistas of creativity or vision. Not once have we together questioned our callings or wrestled with destiny. We can't share a longing for a deeper experience of reality or a transformation of our current situations. She just can't go there. Communicate? Yes. Dialogue? Hardly.

As human beings we've been given the gift of dialogue. This gift goes beyond the simple communication level of Snuggles and enables us to create something of meaning and purpose through conversation. Yet this gift has been largely ignored in recent years, especially in the church. It's as if we've settled for the communication level of Snuggles, when so much more is possible.

Too many church communities and leadership teams are stuck in cyclical chats that rehash yesterday's news or rehearse tomorrow's troubles. But deep down, we're all weary of these chats, and we're hungry for something more. The aim of this book is to reignite the gift of dialogue, which by God's grace will open you and your community to God's possibilities for your church. My desire is to equip you with the skills you will need to turn this kind of creative communication into a reliable and trustworthy practice.

Although this book is about dialogue, it's far more than a collection of communication "tips and techniques." It's also a book that invites leaders and members of churches to reconsider how vision is discovered and expressed. A lot of noise has been made in recent years about the postmodern transition afoot in our culture and about how the vision of churches must change in response to that transition. But most of this noise has not yet translated into much tangible transformation. The ideas in this book will help you move from noise to implementation.

Getting the Most Out of This Book

Some books are best read in community. This is that kind of book. To read this book alone is to miss the underlying idea conveyed in its pages. From cover to cover, the clarion call is an invitation to dialogue. But it's more. *Discovering Your Church's Future Through Dynamic Dialogue* is designed to enable teams and other groups of people in your church to explore and discover vision through the doorway of conversation. The first four chapters will help you understand and apply the concepts of dynamic dialogue, while the second half of the book walks you through five critical issues all churches must converse about if they are to thrive: mission, ministry, motion, money, and method.

A book on dialogue wouldn't be complete without offering significant and specific means by which to enter the conversation. Woven into each chapter are two ways to ignite real conversation: conversation starters and "experiencercises."

Conversation starters are designed to get the energy of your team or community moving toward dialogue. Don't feel that you have to answer every question I've provided. Think of the questions as on-ramps to ideas and concepts that are important to your team or community. The conversation starters are meant to help you, not box you in, so use them as you see fit. However, I would not recommend skipping them altogether. This book is meant to encourage conversation and help it to flourish. And the questions are designed to assist in this process. Use them as you see fit—but use them.

> The experience that each exercise generates will inform the group about its strengths and weaknesses as a team of creative conversationalists.

Experiencercises are group exercises designed to instigate creative conversation. Each exercise is intended to create a dynamic experience within the group, which is the starting point of dialogue. The experience that each exercise generates will inform the group about its strengths and weaknesses as a team of creative conversationalists.

The experiences that emerge from the exercises will be different for each group. Like the conversation starters, the exercises are only on-ramps to the experience. The experiencercises are critical to this book because they help groups understand how to take conversation beyond talk and make it an emergent experience in itself. (An emergent experience is one that may unfold within certain "planned perimeters," but it always yields unexpected ideas, principles, and wisdom.)

Each chapter will include experiencercises that bring the content of the chapter home in a unique way. I encourage you to take the experiencercises seriously (*and* have fun with them) and to be very intentional about including them in your group's time together. Each experiencercise can expand or contract in length depending on how much time you have. Don't eliminate the experiencercise because of time; simply reduce the amount of time you give it. Some of the experiencercises will require a facilitator. When that is the case, I will provide a few thoughts for facilitation.

My hope is that together we will discover authentic dialogue at every level of our church communities: between leaders and members, leaders and other leaders, unpaid leaders and staff leaders, and so on. The gift of dialogue is yours; unwrap it, and discover the treasure that awaits you inside.

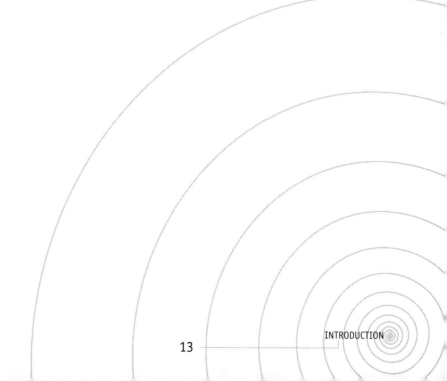

CHAPTER 1

A PLACE TO BEGIN:
Moving Toward Dynamic Dialogue

"All depends on the quality of the conversations."
—Alan Webber

Voice Activated

IN JUNE 2001, the Detroit Free Press published an article informing twenty-first century tech-heads of more good news: Voice-activated technology was about to change our lives for good. Brenda Rios wrote, "In a few years, people will be able to order pizzas over the phone without ever talking to a person, change a TV channel with a word or two and file expense reports or update inventories from their cars by speaking into a cell phone."

Rios explained that major bugs had been worked out of the technology, and it could be a part of mainstream life within five years. The article went on to identify the automobile industry, airlines, communications companies, and "directory assistance" as domains where the technology was already in existence. Two years later, in 2003, more and more voice-activated systems are popping up all around us.

This book is about another kind of voice-activated system—one that is desperately needed in the church today. This voice-activated system creates unity, ownership, and motivation throughout a community. I call it "dynamic dialogue." Dynamic dialogue is a creative process that church leaders and members* enter into in order to discover and express the unique vision God is continually revealing in their midst.

> Dynamic dialogue is a creative process that church leaders and members enter into in order to discover and express the unique vision God is continually revealing in their midst.

---

*I use the word *member* in the sense that the Apostle Paul used it: All Christians are members of the body. It is my way of distinguishing between leaders and lay people. I chose this word because of my distaste for the phrase *lay people,* and because it more accurately reflects what the people of any given church are: members of the body. I recognize leaders are members of the body as well. But some distinction is necessary for this book.

Unfortunately, much of the conversation the church is engaged in has little to do with the adventure of following Jesus or revealing his grace to the world. Step inside a church, and you'll hear all sorts of petty chat about theology, kingdom building (the wrong kingdom!), infighting, scandals, and political agendas. The church often seems more concerned with communicating the fine print of doctrine, belief structures, and acceptable behaviors than with discovering and living the good news in word and in deed. There is no doubt that the "correct," the "proper," and the "safe" have hijacked the grace-filled conversation in many of our churches.

> Unfortunately, much of the conversation the church is engaged in has little to do with the adventure of following Jesus or revealing his grace to the world.

Listen closer, and you'll hear leaders and members trigger all sorts of frustration in one another. Leaders tend to praise the vocally compliant and bemoan those who question, well...anything. Members are not much better. Many complain as if complaining were a spiritual gift, and use their voices to thwart at every turn. Then there are those—both leaders and members—who neither complain nor evoke. Their vocal cords are in perpetual neutral, not wanting to offend or risk.

For some time now, we've settled for these "less than" conversations that prevent true community and diminish genuine creativity. Certainly our vocal cords, and the lives behind those precious instruments, were meant for better conversations—those that lead to vital relationships that speak with creativity and passion. In her book *Turning to One Another,* Margaret J. Wheatley wrote, "I believe we can change the world if

> There is no doubt that the "correct," the "proper," and the "safe" have hijacked the grace-filled conversation in many of our churches.

we start listening to one another again. Simple, honest, human conversation. Not mediation, negotiation, problem-solving, debate, or public meetings. Simple, truthful conversation where we each have a chance to speak, we each feel heard, and we each listen well."

My desire is to invite you to recapture the wonder of this kind of simple yet life-changing conversation. I believe it can permeate every corner of your church and reform the way leaders and members discover and express vision. The dialogue is within our reach and is even our birthright. Why settle for less?

The absence of true dialogue has not happened by accident; it is the result of our current course and speed. In the last few decades, the approach to church has created two trouble spots that

> Leaders and members must perceive each other as vital to the conversation before they will make the space for it to occur.

have minimized the potential for conversation. If we desire to choose a different path for the future, we need to understand these trouble spots and chart a course away from them.

Trouble Spot 1: Leader-Exclusive Vision

Much of what needs to be conversationally reformed revolves around the traditional relationship between leaders and members. For too long, vision has been reserved for leaders. Leaders believed it was their divine right to discover and explain the vision with little or no input from members. And many members obliged this idea. This mindset totally ignores the critical interaction between leaders and members that fosters true vision.

What's needed today is the understanding that this conversational relationship — between leaders and members — is a portal by which vision can be discovered and expressed. This relational shift will yoke leaders and members together in the unearthing of vision through creative dialogue. As with so many things in life, this change will begin first at the level of perception. Leaders and members must perceive each other as vital to the conversation before they will make the space for it to occur.

Conversation Starters

- Do you agree that the church is trapped in far too many "less than" conversations? Name some of these conversations you see afoot in the church in general.

- Let's move a bit closer to home. Where might your church be trapped in these "less than" conversations?

- If you were standing on the outside looking in, what would these "less than" conversations lead you to believe about your church?

- Let's assume that the kind of simple but life-changing dialogue I've described is possible in your church. What obstacles might prevent it from becoming a reality?

This trouble spot cannot be negotiated with the same processes by which we set our present course. Leaders and members will need to embrace *unfamiliar relational spaces* in order to discover new spiritual and conversational lands. Both groups will play an important role in the process of ushering in this relationship, and both will face challenges along the way.

Leaders and members will have to let go of the relational dynamics they know so well, where leaders find the vision and members carry it out. We've become fairly comfortable with that method, but it will not take us where we need to go in the decades ahead. Instead, leaders must learn to share—and at times, even surrender—power. This may run counterintuitive to some current ideas on leadership. But leading like Jabba the Hutt just won't do if conversation is the aim.

> The strong leader of the future is not the keeper of the vision; he or she is the facilitator of its emergence.

Members, on the other hand, must learn to step into the process of dialogue and assume partial responsibility for the discovery of vision. However, this must be done without negating the leader's vantage point or unique gifts. This will require that members learn to discern when to push back on the leader's ideas and when to embrace them. It will require members to be awake and alert throughout the process.

The new dynamics will enable leaders and members to collectively listen to the Spirit and then dialogue their way to the expression of that voice. Moving from the familiar way of doing things will require both groups to enter a time of ambiguity. This is a necessary season in which both will learn to move together in a new way.

There is still a place for strong leaders and followers in dynamic dialogue. However, the strong leader of the future is not the keeper of the vision; he or she is the facilitator of its emergence. Hence, conversation is critical. The vision, breathed by God, resides more in the people than the leader. The leader will draw the vision out of the community where incarnation can occur. In "The Coming of the New Organization," Peter Drucker likens the leader of the future to a conductor of a symphony. Perfect! The conductor engages the orchestra in a conversation that unlocks potential and creates space for something bigger than what he or she could ever express alone.

After twenty years of conducting the Boston Philharmonic Orchestra, Benjamin Zander realized that the vision for a particular piece of music comes from activating the passion locked up in the players. In *The Art of Possibility*, he wrote, "I had been conducting for nearly twenty years when it suddenly dawned on me that the conductor of an orchestra does not make a sound." When he realized that the orchestra members were not incidental to the music-making process, he discovered his desire to engage them in conversation. "But how, actually, could I know what the players were feeling about my effectiveness in releasing their power?...I found I wanted more information, and more relationship. Our eyes meeting across a crowded room was simply not enough; I wanted to hear what they had to say."

Conversation Starters

- What kind of conversations currently dominate the landscape between leaders and members in your church?

- Why don't leaders and members talk about vision? If you do have this conversation at your church, what enables it?

- Do you agree that leaders and members need to change their relationship in order to discover and express vision together?

- Why do you think "vision discovery" has been primarily in the domain of formal leaders?

- If you are a leader, share with the group your fears or concerns about including members in the discovery process.

- If you are a member, share with the group your fears or concerns about being included in the discovery process.

This is exactly the kind of relationship leaders and members need in order to discover the music of their community's unique vision. For the church, creative dialogue does not occur in a musical rehearsal, but in the field of dialogue in which leaders and members meet to uncover and realize what the Spirit is revealing.

Trouble Spot 2:
The Sameness Syndrome

The second trouble spot that has diminished creative conversation between leaders and members is the copycat mentality so prevalent in the church today. Pastors of large and small churches flock to pastors of larger ones to learn why the larger ones got that way and how to do the same (as if bigness were the ultimate goal of the kingdom!). The leaders of the larger churches often plead with the leaders of the smaller churches not to go home and replicate what they're doing, but the seminar participants often do it anyway. The sameness syndrome is alive and well in the name of "not re-creating the wheel." It's time to jettison this fascination with a one-size- or one-purpose-fits-all mentality. As Len Sweet puts it in his book *AquaChurch*, "No two churches are alike. No two pastors are alike. No two ministries are alike. No two people even understand their church the same way. You need a map of your ministry that is as unique as your thumb print."

The simple truth is that it's easier to copy another church's success than it is to dialogue your way to your own. It's easier to listen to a monologue from another pastor telling you about his or her vision than it is to discover your own *with* your members. It's easier to slap on a new, prepackaged model of ministry than it is to dive into the ambiguity of your situation in order to craft something truly unique.

Going to a conference (even as an entire staff), discovering a "vision," and going home to cast it can cause all sorts of problems, not the least of which is the fact that a leader with a prepackaged vision will favor monologue over dialogue. He or she must become a master of "the sell" rather than a facilitator of an adventure.

Now don't abandon me here; I'm not against conferences and the good ideas of others. I agree that leaders should occasionally meet for renewal and rest. But I am weary of the modern church's tendency to mass-produce itself in the name of some "biblical imperative"—which conveniently is the theme of the next conference. I am grateful for the churches that lead the way through innovation and intention. Yet what we can learn from these churches is that innovation and intention—and I believe creative and widespread dialogue (enabled by grace)—brought these churches to *their* destinies. The stories from these successful churches should evoke within other leaders the passion to find, with their members, their own unique stories.

Of course there will be certain things we all hold in common. I'm not suggesting that we shouldn't share ideas and use good ideas from other churches. I guess

Conversation Starters

- Do you agree that the church has adopted a copycat mentality?

- Why do you think we all want to be the same? Share three reasons you believe your church is unique and what you could do to maximize that uniqueness.

we don't have to reinvent *every* wheel. But the body of Christ should have as many diverse expressions as there are human bodies—each unique and yet part of a larger whole. This is not discovered through imitation but rather through dynamic dialogue. The conversation espoused in these pages is meant to help a church find and follow its unique path.

"Sorry, Dave, but I Don't Think So!"

At this point, you may be protesting a bit. If you're a leader, you may be thinking this idea seems impossible because non-staff members don't have the time, desire, or energy for this kind of conversation. Or maybe you think this idea might work in smaller churches but not in mid-sized and larger congregations. Maybe you think members just don't have a grasp of the issues the staff faces every day and would therefore slow the conversation down. Or maybe you believe that the primary element people would bring to the conversation is what they tend to bring now: complaints.

If you're not a part of the formal leadership structure of your church, you might be thinking, "Are you kidding? My pastor(s) would never want to hear what I have to say." Or maybe you've had difficulty with leaders and members alike in your congregation and no longer trust them in any conversation. Perhaps you feel intimidated because you're not "trained" for this kind of conversation and think it should be left to the paid holy people. Or possibly you've tried to initiate such a dialogue and found no takers.

Leaders and members alike may be thinking, "Well, we don't really need this kind of conversation because we already know our vision." And of course at one level this is true. But at another level, I want to encourage you to see the vision of your church as emergent. To suggest your church's vision is fixed would be like suggesting your personal life's vision is complete. Impossible! Life, individually and collectively, unfolds over time. Dialogue enables and reveals that unfolding.

Whatever your objections, I hope to address them in the pages ahead. But for now, I am advocating the idea that leaders and members all need a voice in the creative conversation of your church's emerging vision. I am not calling for nonstaff people to run the church or make all the decisions. But members and leaders (paid staff of all stripes) need to experience electrifying and life-creating conversations that lead them to Jesus and the unfolding of their church's destiny.

SUPPLIES: white board or a large sheet of butcher paper and a marker

INSTRUCTIONS: Review page 21, where I point out some of the reasons leaders and members may not believe this kind of dialogue is possible. Which of those reasons most nearly articulates your concerns? Why?

List the group's reasons for concern on a large piece of butcher paper or a white board. Try to find the common thread in all the concerns. What is the one theme that weaves its way through all the concerns?

Now discuss that one concern from two vantage points. First, discuss why you believe this concern is shared by everyone in the group. Second, discuss what it would take to remove that concern so that the conversation can freely continue. As you discuss what it will take to remove the concern, list those things on another piece of paper. Then narrow down to one word all of your discussion about what would remove the concern. Finally, on another sheet of paper, write on the left-hand side the one word that represents the major concern and on the right-hand side the one word that represents its removal. Here are two examples:

Territorialism	Trust
Power	Stewardship

Now, as you use this book in the days ahead, keep in mind how your group or community must move in order to unleash the conversation.

{ **EXPERIENCE**ercise }

SUPPLIES: white board or a large sheet of butcher paper and markers of many different colors (If you want to save the picture that emerges from the activity, use butcher paper.)

PREPARATION: Before the session, tape a large strip of butcher paper to a smooth wall, and place a wide selection of markers nearby.

CONTEXT: This chapter focuses on the idea that creative conversation helps a community to discover its emerging and unique vision. It helps answer the questions "What is God up to here?" and "What is God up to here, based on the unique people and gifts found in this community?" Learning to identify and steward this emerging vision is part of the conversation.

INSTRUCTIONS: Your group is going to draw two pictures of your church. The first will portray your church today. The second will portray what you believe your church could be in the future. Remember these are group pictures.

Choose one person to begin. The first person can draw whatever he or she would like to get things going, but from that point on, every person must connect what he or she draws to some other part of the picture. In other words, it must all somehow connect. Continue the process until everyone has drawn something. Then continue with rounds of drawing until the group is satisfied that the picture is complete. Toward the end, you may find people hopping up to add a nuance here or there. That's OK.

It's important to stress that the picture, though drawn by many, is to be one picture. It can include "mini-pictures," but the goal is to always connect the separate contributions to the picture so that they ultimately emerge into a whole. Ask participants to express their individual creativity while keeping the collective aim in mind. Each picture should take about fifteen minutes to draw (move quickly, and don't strive for a Picasso). I've seen this work with as many as sixty people, but it works best with about twenty.

Debriefing the EXPERIENCEercise

- What did the first picture tell you about how the group currently views your church?

- What did the second picture tell you about how the group views your church's potential?

- What did you learn about one another as you drew the pictures together?

- How might this experiencercise be similar to discovering your unique and emerging vision as leaders and members?

GROWING GRASS AND
Conversing Creatively

The Dynamics of Discussion

Chuck and I had been friends for about a year when we decided to meet consistently. We had no big agenda in mind. It was just a chance to enjoy each other's company and appreciate each other's vantage point on life and ministry. The meetings usually occurred over lunch or breakfast. To the casual onlooker, these times must have appeared about as interesting as grass growing. But then again, growing grass is quite extraordinary. And at times, so were our discussions.

I could always tell when the conversation was turning extraordinary. Chuck would get this grin on his face, bounce his legs up and down, and make small arm gestures as if he were cheering for his favorite team but didn't want to overdo his enthusiasm. The texture of these moments changed from simple content to *a kind of creation process that was occurring in the moment*. In other words, the conversation was literally reshaping us as we had it. Not only that, but it provided the raw materials necessary for further reshaping at a later time. I often left those simple meetings with a renewed energy to live with passion and purpose.

Over the years, I've experienced conversations similar to those I shared with Chuck. With friends, family members, and colleagues, the grass has grown in extraordinary ways. As more and more of these conversations accumulated in my life, I grew hungrier for them and even disappointed when they didn't materialize. And then I noticed that though these conversations seemed to occur quite spontaneously, a consistent investment of time seemed to enable them. Though they seemed to materialize quite serendipitously, a kind of cultivation increased their likelihood. I began to view this kind of conversation as an art form in which the artists (the conversationalists) had definite roles to play and definite snares to avoid.

I also noticed that these creative conversations could occur in groups—although it seemed more difficult to maintain the necessary space and freedom for the conversation to flourish. Yet when groups had these extraordinary grass-growing conversations, the electricity and potency of the moment seemed even greater than what I experienced one-on-one with friends.

And then, of course, I discovered I wasn't the only person thinking about this stuff.

David Bohm, a quantum physicist, has spent years studying and describing the process of creative conversation that he calls *dialogue*. In "Dialogue—A Proposal," Bohm describes dialogue as a nobler kind of conversation. "Usually people gather either to accomplish a task or to be entertained, both of which can be categorized as predetermined purposes."

Bohm goes on to describe a deeper conversation, not driven by task, entertainment, or teaching: "By its very nature Dialogue is not consistent with any such purposes beyond the interest of its participants in the unfoldment and revelation of the deeper collective meanings that may be revealed."

This kind of dialogue is more art than technique. The conversation itself becomes part of the creative process of discovering and shaping common vision. Bohm puts it this way: "Participants find that they are involved in an ever changing and developing pool of common meaning. A shared content of consciousness emerges which allows a level of creativity and insight that is not generally available to individuals or to groups that interact in more familiar ways." Yes, that's it! That's what made my conversations with Chuck (and so many others) so electrifying. Bohm's description is a wonderful picture of where this journey will take us.

We've been given this wondrous gift of conversation. Through communication we can bring energy, vision, and passion to daily life and communal endeavors. If

{ Conversation Starters

- Share your own stories of creative conversations in which you've participated. How did those moments change you?

- What do you think you can do to cultivate those moments without forcing them?

the church needs anything in the days and years ahead, it needs people who understand the necessity of shaping a conversation that leads to creative expressions of God's grace and God's passion to communicate his love to the world he created.

CHAPTER **2**

SPACE MAKERS:
Creating Space for the QUEST

The Space Between Us

"I JUST DON'T FEEL LIKE I'M CONNECTING with the team. In fact, I'm not even sure if I'm still *on* the team." Jonathan had attended North Way Christian Community for about two years. He and I had hit it off with a kind of energy similar to what Chuck and I experienced. Our lives, though different in many ways, converged around a number of important commonalities. One of those shared passions was the desire to help people discover the riches of spiritual formation and the practices that bring those riches to life.

Because of this shared passion, Jonathan almost immediately began serving in the spiritual formation ministries that I oversee at North Way. He taught classes and developed video curriculum for our small groups. All seemed well until Jonathan described his disconnected feeling to my colleague. He had begun to feel distant from the team, like an errand boy of sorts—doing his duty but not fulfilling his dreams or desires. It seemed as though he had no *voice* to help shape the ministry—at least not beyond the one we gave him, or allowed him.

I have to admit that my first thought upon hearing of Jonathan's discontent was emotional heartburn. "Oh great, this is going to take time to figure out—time I don't have." It felt like the moment early on in putting a puzzle together—after all the easy pieces are connected and it starts to get hard. "Why can't Jonathan just be happy? Look what he's doing for us." My next thought was even more selfish. "What if he stops doing what he's doing for us?" I was put out with myself for having that thought, as if I were a kind of spiritual godfather trying to keep the "family" together. Yikes.

My colleague suggested to Jonathan that the three of us meet to discuss the situation. Once I got over my selfish godfather thing, the meeting became dynamic and yielded the beginnings of a new role, a new voice, for Jonathan. The voice would bring him squarely into a conversation that up to that point had been reserved for paid team members. In other words, we brought him onto the paid spiritual formation staff and just left the "paid" part out.

What's important to realize in this story is that nothing of significance would have occurred among the three of us without an *intentional creation of space*. My emotional heartburn was caused by the reality that the situation at hand would need space and grace—two things you can't just stuff into a quick discussion and hope for the best. Jonathan's new role on the team would not have emerged without the space we created to discover it. Mark this well: Dynamic discussions require intentional space for discovery, discernment, and creativity.

> **Dynamic discussions require intentional space for discovery, discernment, and creativity.**

Peer into the Creation account in Genesis, and you'll discover space— lots of it! Space gave everything else a place to exist. Space was (and is) the canvas of creation. Conversational space makes intentional room for spontaneous insights to emerge. As leaders and members talk about purpose and vision, they must create this kind of space. It is the down payment that initiates the dialogue.

What's a Group to Do in the Space: The QUEST

Once the space is created, other elements become important to the conversation. Without these necessary components, all the conversation in the world—spontaneous or intentional—will not lead to dynamic dialogue. Because these elements are so critical to the success of the conversation, we will spend the rest of this chapter discovering these ingredients and weaving them into a process model I call the QUEST.

It's important to remember that models are most helpful when they provide us with a framework to discover our hearts and the rich content available to us in creative dialogue. Don't

Conversation Starters

- Share a time that making space for dialogue changed the course of your life or ministry.

- Describe some of the consequences of not making space for dialogue, particularly with regard to ministry issues.

let the model take the place of the heart or the content. As often overly rationalistic Westerners, we are famous for replacing heart with technique. When we do this, we lose the very thing we hoped the model would help us find: life.

The goals of the QUEST are the QUEST itself and where it takes you and your fellow conversationalists. You are like the mighty Bilbo Baggins and his companions who set off to kill the dragon and find the gold in *The Hobbit*. It is important to see creative conversation as a journey or an adventure. If we reduce it to mere technique, than we dull the process and the potential outcome.

You can visualize this QUEST in a number of ways. You can see it as a linear journey, where you begin with the first step and move through the process from one step to the next. Or you can view the model as circular. From this vantage point, the process may begin at any point and move in a circular fashion. And, for those most radical among us, you can view it as process-free. In this case you would view each item in the model as part of a stew—you never know what combination will surface when you bring your spoon out of the bowl. Regardless of the way you view it, I hope that the elements in the QUEST will give the members of your group a vehicle that will move them closer to knowledge and wisdom.

> "If you want to figure out your path in life, you can't have an end date on the exploration."—*John Wood, founder of a nonprofit group that builds libraries for children in Asia*

Q—Question

There is a scene in the movie *The Matrix* when Trinity first meets Neo and begins to awaken him to something at work deep in his sterile existence. She whispers in his ear, "It's the question that drives us." What a perfect description of what questions accomplish in dynamic dialogue!

In the modern world, questions have been reduced to nothing more than preludes to answers. Once the answer has been determined, the question is no longer necessary. There is a place for this kind of closed questioning, but the art of conversation requires that we view questions (and questioning) as tools of exploration rather than as temporary impediments to solutions.

> The question is like a shovel you thrust into the ground to break up the surface.

In creative dialogue, the question is like a shovel you thrust into the ground to break up the surface. Once the ground of the dialogue is broken open, the real exploration can begin. I'm not suggesting that answers will not come, but our propensity for the quick answer shields us from the power of the question. When our curiosity is satisfied by one answer, the conversation will last only as long as it takes to find that one answer. Most questions of vision have a potential for several veins of exploration. And as a group, you need to explore those veins.

I was recently helping a team explore the primary heartbeat of its collective vision. The more questions the group asked, the more possibilities surfaced that had to be considered. As more questions and possibilities surfaced, a collective frustration surfaced as well. At that point, I tried to help the group understand the absolute appropriateness of questioning and searching. I assured them that at the right time, the "way" would reveal itself with the clarity necessary to help them move forward. What the group needed was permission to question its world without rushing to a premature solution.

Questions produce a communal yearning. We need to learn to let those yearnings grow. From that yearning will come a kind of energy that sustains the early stages of creative dialogue. The yearning produces a sense of adventure and a willingness to pursue that adventure.

Conversation Starters

- Do you agree that we are prone to see a question as little more than the prelude to an answer?

- Share a time in your life or ministry when you rushed to answer a question and didn't allow it to lead you to exploration. What was the result?

- Share a current question you're facing in life or ministry. What areas of life or ministry is that question leading you to explore?

- Can you identify a collective yearning in your community? How would you describe that yearning? What do you think that yearning is inviting your community to explore?

SUPPLIES: markers and a white board or large sheet of paper

INSTRUCTIONS: On a white board or large sheet of paper, write the collective yearning you identified in the last Conversation Starter. Next, ask as many questions related to that yearning as you can. Try to come up with at least twenty-five questions that are related to that initial communal yearning. Then identify commonalities in the questions. What are all the questions revealing about the collective yearning? At this point, try to explore the yearning through these questions. Don't rush to a solution.

U—UNEARTH

The questioning process breaks up the ground and yields important ideas. These ideas can then be unearthed and examined for important messages. These messages are not only important to the emergent vision but also to the health of the group or community. These unearthed messages narrow the information into patterns and principles.

Patterns: Haven't We Been Here Before?

As groups QUEST, they will inevitably unearth patterns that reveal bits and pieces about who they are and how they relate. These patterns will reveal both bright and blind spots at work in the group. All communities and teams inevitably form both healthy and dysfunctional patterns. Once formed, those patterns in turn shape the community. When groups enter a dynamic discussion, they will discover these patterns. Some of these patterns will need to go, and some will need to grow. Discerning which is which is critical to the conversation and well-being of the group.

In their book *Seven Life Lessons of Chaos,* authors John Briggs and F. David Peat describe the patterns that occur in nature known as fractals. They write, "The word was coined by the mathematician Benoit Mandelbrot and now has wide use in chaos theory, where fractals refer to the traces, tracks, marks, and forms made by the action of chaotic dynamical systems." These fractals, or patterns, are the result of nature interacting with itself, if you will. A river creates fractals as it cuts its way through a dry channel. A storm produces a swirling fractal that is not detected from the ground but is evident from space.

I like to think of a group's patterns as fractals. The unearthing phase of the QUEST provides the group the possibility of finding and naming the patterns. Naming patterns is far more than assigning labels. It means a group is able to describe the fractal and how it has influenced its interactions. The members of the group can further determine if the fractal will be important to their future or if it should be eliminated. The fractal name becomes an icon of sorts that represents the fractal (and the behavior behind it) and allows the group to easily refer to and understand the newly discovered pattern.

I worked with a church that had reached a plateau it couldn't seem to move beyond. As we peered into the culture, it was evident that the success of the church had been built on independent, entrepreneurial people who developed ministries somewhat in isolation. This fractal had been repeated so many times that now the church was full of island patterns. These islands were strong, department-like ministries that had lost connection to the overarching purpose of the church. Many successful islands had led to a number of important but disconnected ministries. This pattern was unearthed in the quest to discover what had contributed to the plateau and what God was saying to this community through that plateau.

You can talk all day about vision, but if the health of your team or community is in question, the conversation will always stall. Dynamic dialogue is more than discussions that lead to new vision. It is also the way by which the team appraises its condition and takes steps to increase its vitality. The two—health and vision—work hand in hand. The island church's discovery of a dysfunction in its structure eventually

Conversation Starters

- Describe three group patterns you've identified on your team or in your church. Try to come up with a metaphor (such as the island ministry) for the fractal.

- What do these patterns tell you about your team or church?

- How will these patterns move you closer to or away from your emerging vision?

- Can you verbalize a principle that emerges from the patterns you've identified? Try to word the principle in a short phrase you can remember.

- What does this principle tell you about your emerging vision?

led to the next part of the church's communal vision.

Health and vision work hand in hand.

Principles

Principles are bits and pieces of reality (revealed truth) that normally surface as a result of discovering group patterns. These principles often take the shape of an "aha moment." We'll look at the aha moment more closely when we examine the "s" in QUEST. For now, remember that the power of a principle is that it expresses a truth the group will need as it moves forward. First come the patterns, then come the principles that elaborate on and explain the patterns.

The "island church" discovered that the next piece of vision would require it to reconnect all its separate islands into one large continent where diversity and synergy would become partners. It was no longer enough to sacrifice synergy for a diverse ministry; both virtues were needed. Learning to synergize and yet honor diversity became part of the emerging vision. However, until this idea was expressed in a principle— "Our value of diversity can no longer trump our need for synergy" —it could not be actualized throughout the community. Localizing and vocalizing patterns increase the likelihood of real change.

E—ENCOUNTER

As I work with teams in my consulting practice, it never ceases to amaze me how easy it is for individuals on teams to take each other's presence for

> "All actual life is encounter."
> —Martin Buber

granted. The specific people in the conversation are often viewed as either incidental or downright unimportant. The next part of the QUEST helps you understand your vision in light of the people who are part of the dialogue.

Have you ever wondered why the people in your life are in your life? Oh, I know on bad days we wonder that. But that's not what I mean. Certainly we can reject the notion that the people closest to us are there by accident or coincidence. Think of it this way: Out of all the time periods you could have been born, you are alive now. Out of all the places where you could have been born and grown up, you were born and grew up in the places you did. And think of all the zigs and zags in your life. Think of all the places you've been

Have you ever wondered why the people in your life are in your life?

and choices you've made that have led you to the group of people who now live and serve alongside you in your church community.

Now, with all that in mind, consider those people. Think of their histories and choices and all it took to get all of you in the same location at the same time. *Out of the six billion people you could have ended up with, you've all landed together.* Amazing! How could we ever, therefore, take those around us as incidental to the conversation and emerging vision? But we do. I am convinced that a group, at least in part, discovers its collective vision as its members encounter one another and realize that the conversation will be shaped by those unique encounters. The "who" of your team will shape the "what" of your vision.

> The "who" of your team will shape the "what" of your vision.

In 1992 my family and I moved to Maryland to help plant a church. A handful of passionate people formed a core group that longed to launch a distinctive kind of church in the Washington, D.C. area. The leader and his wife invited my family and me to join them in this venture. By the time we arrived, David and Diane had already been hard at work nurturing a small group of people who all shared a common vision. Not long after our arrival, another couple joined our team to work with students. The "who" was coming together.

The group did whatever it took to move the fledgling church forward. Most of us worked second (and sometimes third) jobs to support families and the endeavor. Soon there were fifteen to twenty of us who were sold on the mission. We met weekly to worship, grow, and shape the vision. Occasionally we drew sixty or seventy people who seemed interested in our kind of church. Our early successes seemed to suggest we were on our way to establishing a true critical mass that would form the core needed to launch the church. Our committed core continued to meet, adding a new person here and there while preparing to "go public."

During those "house church days"—prior to our formal launch—the committed core grew close as friends and ministry partners. As we got to know one another, we discovered that each of us had just come out of a rather wounded period in his or her life. The intimate nature of the group allowed us to bring tremendous support and healing to one another. But we were always careful to maintain an outward focus so that our mission would remain clear—to plant a new kind of church in the D.C. area. There was only one problem. The more we focused on "our" vision to plant a church, the more that vision seemed to elude us. On a number of occasions, we seemed close to our dream, but we never achieved the necessary lift. What was going on?

As all church planters know, there is a moment in the endeavor when you have to fish or cut bait. If momentum dies, you eventually have to move on. Some two years into the process, we reached that point. As we faced the reality that the church was not to be, it became clear that we had been brought together from around the United States to help one another heal, rather than to plant a church. It took some time for us to all believe this enough to embrace it. Perhaps some who were part of that core would not completely agree with my evaluation, but we had to watch a dream end.

Conversation Starters }

- Do you agree that it's easy to miss how the people in a community or on a team shape the vision?

- How would your ideas about vision change if you believed each person on the team or in the community holds a part of the emerging vision? How would this change the way you view others?

- If your group is fairly small, take some time to share something from your journey that the group may not know about you.

- How does this new piece of information change the way you view others in your group?

- What might these pieces of information (bits of group members' stories) tell you about your emerging vision?

I do believe that most of that core group of people would agree with me that our emergent purpose was partially, if not predominantly, determined by the "who" of the group. It was no coincidence that we were all wounded and broken and in need of healing. It was no accident that we were able to minister healing to one another. And it was no coincidence that the health that was achieved in that group readied all of us to go on to unique and powerful ministries around the country and the world.

My days in D.C. taught me that you can't separate your emerging vision from the emerging encounters of those involved in the conversation. I'm not suggesting that most dynamic conversations and encounters will lead to dissolution. Hardly. But I am advocating that the people and their current places in life have much to do with the emerging vision of your community. That's why they're there! Don't underestimate the ongoing encounter and what it is telling you.

> Don't underestimate the ongoing encounter and what it is telling you.

{ EXPERIENCEercise }

SUPPLIES: a 100-piece puzzle

INSTRUCTIONS: Select ten people from the group, and give each person ten pieces of the puzzle. Give the team fifteen minutes to put as much of the puzzle together as possible.

Debriefing the EXPERIENCEercise

Ask participants to discuss the experience. What obstacles and frustrations did they encounter? What did it teach them about working together? Relate the experiencercise to discovering a collective vision. How is it similar and different?

S—SERENDIPITY

The ancient Greeks used two different words to describe the concept of time. The first is *chronos*. *Chronos* is probably the word we are more familiar with because of its usage in many of our time-oriented words, such as *chronometer* and *chronological*. The second word is *kairos*. We must familiarize ourselves with this concept if we desire creative dialogue. It's a word rich in texture and subtlety. *Kairos* is "an invitation to seize an opportunity born in eternity that is looking for a home in time." It is a moment of "aha" or serendipity granted you and/or your community by God. Yet, it is *only a possibility* until you decide to harness your energy to *see it* and *birth it* into *this* world. These "*kairos* moments" can seem dramatic or quite ordinary. But there is really nothing ordinary about them. They are invitations from God to see the world anew and to bring shape to it through this newfound awareness and encounter.

At some point in the QUEST, enough ground has been explored and examined that the moment becomes serendipitous. It bursts forth, if you will. This is the moment in the conversation in which enough of the emerging vision has become clear so that the group can see it and then garners its energy to seize it.

Back to the island church for a moment...

The island insight came somewhat serendipitously for the island church. A significant amount of conversation had already taken place among members of the church's senior leadership. What the senior leaders were discovering was good, but I suggested it wasn't good enough. The entire staff needed a chance to enter the conversation and, at some point and in some fashion, the members would need to be engaged as well.

I was leading the staff of the church through a round of conversations about the church's culture. Interestingly, the participants had separated into island groupings during the course of the meetings. In one of the early team conversations, one of the senior leaders happened to remark, "You know, it's like we're a group of islands. We spend a lot of time refereeing disputes among the islands and trying to coordinate schedules and priorities between the islands. But it can get pretty lonely on an island. It can also be hard to sense you're part of something bigger than your own island. I think we've forgotten that we are all really on the same team."

The reaction of the participants revealed to me that this leader had hit the nail on the head. The entire team resonated with the epiphany and added insights to the island metaphor. We consultants pray for this kind of moment because it crystallizes the struggle in a very powerful way. The serendipitous nature of the aha only further enforces its potency. The journey of this team was moving toward this kairos moment long before I showed up. When the leader verbalized the island concept, it was not simply an idea that came from an isolated conversation. Rather, it was a powerful icon that expressed years of history and brought that history into focus.

From that point on, the island metaphor made its way into every team conversation. It became a powerful symbol that enabled the church to make the corrections needed to unite the islands. What's important to recognize is the fact that the island insight was part of the emerging vision for this church. They had discovered a piece of what was to come. From that new place, more and more of the vision surfaced.

As a group or community, you never know when or how the aha moment will emerge. But when it does, seize it! It's an opportunity waiting to be born. It's a piece of your community's unique destiny, and it leads to the final piece of the QUEST.

Conversation Starters

- Share an aha moment your team or church has experienced in its history.

- Do you think your team or church is on the verge of a *kairos* moment? Describe what God might be surfacing that he wants you to seize.

- How do you think God is inviting you to participate in the birthing of this piece of your vision?

T—TRANSFORMATION

The QUEST process eventually leads to transformation. Recognizing the emergent adventure will always lead both the individuals and the entire community to new places of life, growth, and change. Remember, dynamic dialogue is more than creative language; it is creative living and ministry.

When this transformation occurs, it is important to notice it and celebrate it. Since the QUEST is never completed, we don't celebrate arrival; we celebrate God's unfolding purpose and the reformation that comes along with it. As we celebrate what has emerged, we also create a sense of anticipation for what is yet to come. The adventure continues.

Conversation Starters

- Take a few moments to share some memories of your church's adventure so far. Celebrate what God has done and what the members have shared. How has the adventure changed you individually and as a group? Dream about the adventure ahead!

INTERMISSION

AS YOU QUEST, DON'T FORGET THIS

Before I came to North Way Christian Community in 1994, a terribly broken time in my life had led to a dark night of the soul and then to a season of great conversion. (If only it had been as easy to live those days as it is to write about them now!) During the wonderfully difficult days preceding my arrival at North Way, I lost and found my faith again and again—something I occasionally need to do.

Through the deep conversion that occurred before I arrived at North Way, I stumbled upon the contemplative tradition of Christianity. These monks, mothers, fathers, and mystics brought me closer to God, who is always calling us into the conversation.

This season and the faith traditions I discovered had a profound effect on my faith and my ideas about ministry, and I showed up at North Way a rather unusual breed of pastor. (That's putting it mildly. What I read for nourishment made some people twitch and others secretly sneak a peek for themselves. Some wanted to have a good old-fashioned book burning—with guitars and "Kum ba yah"—while others vicariously lived out their own more radical desires through me.) I never overtly tried to sway anyone to accept my views, but neither did I try to hide my unconventional approach to faith. My viewpoints were (and still are) a bit off the beaten path.

At first, North Way wasn't sure what to do with me. Actually, that's probably still the case. What I found at North Way, though, is a group of people who appreciated my differences—even though they did not fully understand or even agree with all of them. I was accepted as the odd bird I was, and still am. I became the resident monk and radical who could always be counted on to say something...well, so nonevangelical. But my viewpoints were respected and would often change the direction of decisions. Space was even made for me to share some of these odd thoughts with the community.

My acceptance into the community of North Way as a different bird is not the end of this story. Because you see, as much as I appreciated the space I was given to express my uniqueness, I was also challenged to examine my radical ways and be sure I wasn't losing touch with "essence issues." I found a wonderful rhythm at North Way. On the one hand, I was given the freedom to explore and to share my explorations in appropriate ways. On the other hand, I was exhorted to temper my more radical, "angsty" side with a communal wisdom that was bigger than my own exploration. I was free to roam, but with certain boundaries in mind. Oh, sometimes I crossed right over those boundaries. But the kind of community I've found at North Way helps me come back to certain essence issues that define my faith and keeps me from crafting a purely relativistic approach to life.

As I look back on my journey in this community, I notice that it has always been the *pool of common meaning*—anchored in Christ—coupled with the appreciation of diversity that allowed me (and others) to roam freely and yet freely return home.

> Until we honor each other's unique path and viewpoint, we cannot truly converse.

I share all of that to say this: North Way and I have been in a conversation for almost ten years. It is a conversation that has honored diversity and held to a common pool of meaning. I have been shaped in so many positive ways through this rhythm. And I believe I have, at least at times, helped to shape this community into a more rounded faith expression of Jesus. And much of this has occurred because of a space between us—between North Way and myself—that was created so that the dialogue of faith could occur freely and consistently.

This gift of common meaning and honored diversity is the prerequisite for dynamic discussion. Before we can go any further in this dynamic dialogue, it's necessary to focus on the space between us and the kind of respect required to meet each other in this space with authenticity and possibility. Until we honor each other's unique path and viewpoint, we cannot truly converse.

On the other hand, before it is possible to delve deeply into the specifics of this conversation, it is necessary to discover what we hold in common. We are so good at drawing lines and labeling one another that anything universal between us is lost. This produces a segregated view of the world. We find ourselves restricting the pool of people with whom we will converse until there are only a few left in our circles of conversation. This is part of what is wrong with evangelicalism today, but that is another conversation.

Respecting our differences and uniqueness while passionately circling around what we share is the prerequisite for dynamic dialogue. It is so important that I encourage groups to occasionally reaffirm those treasures that make their groups what they are and what they can become. From this place of unique and common ground, we can then be open to each other in the hope that we will find together what we could never discover alone. More than that, we will find that what we discover can only be implemented through the unique gifts found in the group. What an amazing conversation!

CHAPTER 3

SABOTAGE POINT:
I Can't Hear You

When the Enemy Is Us

WE SAT ACROSS FROM EACH OTHER over lunch. He was lamenting the fact that recently he had put on a few pounds and just couldn't seem to get the excess weight off. This was bothering him because his weight had never been a problem; he felt uncertain about both the culprit behind the weight gain and the strategy for losing it. So in his frustration, he added more ketchup to his fries.

Let's face it: Human beings sabotage. It's the way we are. It's intriguing that we tend to sabotage what matters most to us. This creates double trouble. Not only do we experience the consequences of the sabotage, but we also have a less positive attitude toward the aspect of life we've sabotaged. Like my friend, for example, when we overeat, sometimes we become frustrated about our ability to lose weight and decide to eat even more.

Sabotage can also undo dynamic dialogue. Whether we intend to or not, we find many ways to thwart creative conversation. In this chapter and the next, I'll describe two major sabotage points and ways to avoid them.

More Than Words

The first way we sabotage conversation is through poor communication. It is impossible to unleash the full power of creative dialogue without good communication skills. In this chapter we will look at essential group communication skills that sharpen the QUEST.

I've spent countless hours in consulting and counseling environments. Over the years, I've discovered that we all have a propensity to pay more attention to the content of our communication than we do to its process. In other words, we talk about the "what" more than we understand the ramifications of the "how." Couples argue over issues of parenting or money (the what), but miss the damaging effects of disgusted looks or tones (the how). The "how" of communication can subtly erode relationships—even when surface agreement is achieved.

Teams or groups will often passionately discuss agenda items (the what) but overlook the unhealthy roles individuals play (the how) in those discussions. Or they overlook the unspoken dynamics of the conversation that thwart health and momentum. I'm not suggesting that content is unimportant. But content is usually the safer element in the conversation. It's easier to spend time on content, almost to the exclusion of process. Consider this example.

> The "how" of communication can subtly erode relationships—even when surface agreement is achieved.

John's been the senior pastor at his church for five years. The members and other leaders appreciate his passion for and dedication to the ministry. But there's a problem. Leaders and members alike have noticed that when John is challenged about ministry ideas or directional issues, he becomes hurt and despondent. It's not long before he begins to question his own leadership ability and the loyalty of those who challenged him. Steve, the youth pastor, is always frustrated because John reminds him of his mother. Sally, an elder at the church and a therapist by vocation, believes John must have had issues with *his* mother.

This dynamic has occurred so many times that it is now a pattern. As soon as John is challenged, the dance begins. He gets hurt and plays the "loyalty card." Those challenging him assure him that they are dedicated and only want to help him and the church thrive. John can't see it.

Conversation Starters

• Can you describe a part of your group's process that inhibits growth and/or collaboration? Remember, we're not talking about content here; we're talking about process. Think of the example of John and his team.

This is a group pattern that not only wastes precious time but also has created a zone of undiscussable topics. "It's just better to agree with John or do what needs to be done without telling him about it," explains Sara, the church's worship director. All of this produces a team with poor communication skills and no apparent way out. The dynamics of this example are process-driven rather than content-driven. The content of the conversations only reveals the process problem—the dance between John and the team. What's this team, this community, to do?

The team needs new skills to help it move into the world of process. The sections that follow reveal the skills and practices that make such a movement possible.

{ EXPERIENCE~ercise~ }

SUPPLIES: enough blindfolds for your entire team minus one

INSTRUCTIONS: This activity requires a group of seven to ten people. One person from the team will facilitate the experi-encercise and therefore must not be blindfolded.

Blindfold the team members, and spin them gently a few times to disorient them. Then place them at different locations in the room so that they can hear, but not touch, one another. The participants' goal is to move from their separate locations and join in one spot in the room. Once there, members of the group must form a triangle within fifteen minutes.

Debriefing the EXPERIENCE~ercise~

- What general insights did you gain about your group's process throughout the exercise?

- In what ways did the team demonstrate frustration?

- What enabled your team to break through those frustrations?

- What group dynamics did you notice occurring among the individuals on the team?

SKILL 1: HOLDING CREATIVE TENSION

It's never a straight line from desire to completion. This is one of the most powerful principles I've discovered in my life, relationships, and calling. Linear thinking and living have a place, but they're never the total picture. As we've already seen, life is a dynamic unfolding—a becoming—more than it is a static or completed picture.

Our collective endeavors are as emergent as our individual ones. Therefore, it goes without saying that the art of conversation will not always move along straight lines, but in loops and layers of chaos, creativity, and clarity. Because of this, learning how to hold the creative tension of ambiguity is necessary for the conversation to flourish. Unfortunately, groups are often uncomfortable with creative tension.

Most of us have a love-hate relationship with creativity. Groups and communities grow weary of the uncertainty that goes along with creativity because they are driven by the need to control agendas and accomplish goals.

> **Learning how to hold the creative tension of ambiguity is necessary for the conversation to flourish.**

But dynamic conversation requires groups to move in the ebbs and flows of creative tension. I believe that true group creativity is wanting in our world, at least in part, due to the fact that few groups cultivate this skill.

When groups hit pockets of resistance and ambiguity in the QUEST, it's easy to view the conversation as an impractical waste of time and give up. It may feel like watching an hour of static on TV. Of course, the opposite can just as easily occur. Some groups that hit ambiguity or chaos in their QUESTs can comfortably wander forever, never landing anywhere. These groups search only for the channels that *have* static.

Dismissing the conversation as impractical or using it as a way to escape clarity reveals a group dysfunction that, at its root, is the same. The dysfunction is laziness. Lazy groups don't want to do the hard work of finding and following their collective calling. They can manifest this laziness through appearing busy and unable to invest the time it would take to discuss issues. However, laziness can also look like over-analysis that never heads in any particular direction. When this is the case, groups wander aimlessly because they don't want to commit.

What causes groups to dismiss or flounder in the conversation? I believe a lot of it comes down to their inability to marshal the power of creative tension. When a team or community is unable to relax and stay with ambiguity, it loses an opportunity to discover vision within the chaos, which is usually where vision is hiding. Learning to cultivate this skill comes when the group can spot the tension and persevere in it rather than avoid or exacerbate it.

Parker Palmer, in his book *Let Your Life Speak,* describes a time he was rappelling off a mountain with a group from Outward Bound. At one point he got stuck and couldn't find a way to rappel beyond a tricky spot on the mountain. He describes hanging there in frustration and fear and this conversation with his instructor:

" 'Parker, is anything wrong?'

"In a high, squeaky voice, I said, 'I don't want to talk about it.'

"...But then she shouted ten words I hope never to forget, words whose impact and meaning I can still feel: 'If you can't get out of it, get into it!' "

Each group experiences similar moments in its collective climb. Tension mounts as the group stalls because of a tricky spot in the QUEST. But like Palmer, groups and churches

> Groups and churches must learn to get into what they cannot get out of.

must learn to get into what they cannot get out of. It is in this collective surrender that the way is often made. Fighting their way through will only produce more trouble. Learning to relax and move deeper into the ambiguity provides the pathway to a better place.

SKILL 2: GROUP SCULPTING

Imagine for a moment that the early part of the conversational QUEST is similar to the early stages of sculpting a statue. In this analogy, the group of conversational artists would first discover a somewhat formless block of emergent vision. Then would come the process of chipping away at the marble to discover the form hidden beneath.

Too many conversations are not dynamic because participants do not view the group as a collection of artists working on the *same* sculpture. They don't work toward the same sculpture; rather they try to sculpt their own ideas and force those ideas on the group or

Conversation Starters

• How do you think your team or church responds when it faces uncertainty?

• How skillful is your group at holding creative tension in order to discover what treasure and vision lie beneath it?

• Would you describe your team as more prone to avoid ambiguity or wander aimlessly in it? Explain and illustrate your answer.

• What skill do you think your team needs most in order to learn to hold creative tension during ambiguity?

• Describe a "tricky spot" in the QUEST your team or church has encountered. Are you finding it difficult to relax into this ambiguity?

• What would it look like if you could embrace this tricky spot instead of avoiding it?

community. This is a *process mistake*. The goal of each individual—in the collective—is to help the community find and fashion its *shared* sculpture, not simply to display his or her own work.

Group sculpting requires people to bring certain conversational tools to the process. In the following sections, we'll examine the purpose and practice of each set of these tools. Our use of these tools will increase if we can appreciate the difference between brainstorming (a facet of dialogue) and discussion. Brainstorming is driven by exploration, emergence, and discovery. When we brainstorm, we explore together without reaching hard and fast conclusions. Discussion, on the other hand, connotes "a pounding out of ideas." In discussion, we bring shape and form to the emergent vision we discovered during our brainstorming. Brainstorming and discussion work together to move a group forward. As vision emerges in brainstorming, it can then be shaped and reshaped through discussion.

This distinction is important because groups must discern when it is time to move from exploration to a deliberate shaping of vision. Some groups, not understanding the power of brainstorming, pound too quickly on an idea that is not ready to be shaped, while other groups explore vision but never commit to its realization through discussion and application. They literally brainstorm a vision to death. Knowing when and how to use both brainstorming and discussion is part of the art of conversation. The following tools will help a group to make the transition from brainstorming to discussion.

Listening and Contributing for Understanding

Those who teach good listening skills have always encouraged people to truly understand the vantage point of the speaker. This communicates to the speaker a sense of being heard and honored. The tool of group listening and contributing for understanding takes this traditional listening skill to a deeper level.

When the individuals in a group truly contribute heartfelt ideas and listen to one another with that same heart, they surely feel respect. However, this pulsating rhythm—contributing and listening—will often also yield the next part of the vision in need of shaping. Remember my friend Chuck? During those grass-growing conversations, I often sensed that we were "onto something," but neither of us knew exactly what we were onto. Then, the more we contributed and listened ("ebbed and flowed" with each other), the more likely it was that the important something would surface. When it did, we achieved a new level of understanding. The aha moment came about because we both contributed and we both listened. When groups reach this kind of understanding, it is as if another piece of the block falls away, allowing more of the form to become apparent.

Imagine the tool of listening as the chisel and the tool of contributing as the hammer. Both tools work in concert to achieve the desired form. The people involved in the sculpting will learn that their discussions will include times when some contribute while others listen. Then, based on what one has contributed, another who has listened will add to that contribution. And then another and another, until group understanding is achieved. The aha moment will surface.

This process must occur again and again in the discussion just as a sculptor taps again and again with the hammer and chisel until the shape appears. Groups fail in sculpting because they don't understand how to listen and contribute. Some groups never truly listen and only contribute. This leads to a mass of information that has no form. Others may listen but rarely contribute. This leads to a less than full form because important vantage points are missing. The first aim of discussion is to allow form to emerge from the block of dialogue. But that is only the first step. After the initial form emerges, the discussion becomes more refined and leads to the next set of tools.

Identifying and Narrowing

The tools of identifying and narrowing further refine the shape of creative conversation and the emerging vision. Groups that can't find appropriate language to express vision end up with half-baked ideas that rarely lead to lasting change. Finding the right language to express the vision is the role of identifying and narrowing. These tools refine vision so it is accessible to the group and to others who may enter the conversation at a later date. It also helps members of the existing group to understand how to maximize and steward their energy in order to manifest that vision.

I once worked with a team whose members felt their senior leader was too heavily involved in the day-to-day operations of the ministry. Imagine that! He agreed that his modus operandi was to micromanage his team out of a desire to provide stability and lessen the potential for failure. Both the team and the leader recognized this problem before inviting me into the process. In other words, they had already contributed and listened enough to identify the issue. I soon discovered that the team had not used the tools of identifying and narrowing to determine why changing this dynamic was critical to the team's success.

As I entered the conversation, I asked the participants to share a bit of the history of the ministry. As they shared, each one pointed to the work of the senior leader as the reason the ministry had reached its current level of effectiveness. I then asked them what would have to change in order for the ministry to reach a new level of effectiveness. The micromanagement issue immediately surfaced. Members of the team shared their frustration, and so did the senior leader. The tension was evident, but everyone involved seemed willing to move forward.

Then I said, "So, if I'm hearing you correctly, this micromanagement thing is not just a nuisance for all concerned; it's actually holding you back from moving to your next level. You can't get to a new place as a team and a ministry from here, right?" After a bit of silence, the team responded affirmatively and expressed how the current structure was stifling the ministry's potential. This was the identification and narrowing the team needed in order to choose a new path. It was not

{ Conversation Starters

- How would your group's conversation change if you viewed it as a group sculpture?

- Do you find your group is full of personal agendas that thwart discovering that "one voice" you need to sculpt together?

- How could you transform personal agendas into each person's unique contribution to the process of vision discovery?

- The first set of tools your team needs includes listening and contributing. Which of these two tools is harder for your team to use? Why?

- What does your group need to cultivate in order to begin using the missing tool?

- Tell about a time your group used the tools of listening and contributing to gain new understanding, allowing a new piece of the vision to emerge.

- The second set of tools includes identifying and narrowing. Which of these two tools is harder for your team to use?

- Is your group good at finding the right language to express what it discovers? Do you find that your group creates solid "language anchors" that are easy to refer to at a later time?

enough to understand the problem of micromanagement. The team had to identify it as the "something" holding it back. Once that was done, there was sufficient energy to make a change. Neither the team nor the senior leader wanted to do anything to paralyze the ministry. When the frustration caused by the current structure was identified as a major inhibitor, the team and the leader could move forward. As long as the micromanagement issue was nothing more than a frustration, the team was powerless to change it. But when I narrowed the issue and linked it to the future success of the ministry, clarity and energy for change emerged.

Groups often choose not to use the tools of identifying and narrowing. Many believe that once a new piece of vision has surfaced through contributing and listening, the conversational process is over, and they move right to implementation. The trouble is that without this second set of tools, the emerging idea is not sufficiently linked to the present and future of the team. Excited to try something new, the team does not pay the price of understanding "why" the "what" has emerged. Without this second round of reflection, teams end up implementing ideas without counting the cost of those ideas. They simply put another addition on the house. Refining new ideas and vision allows a team to integrate those ideas in light of both the realities of the present and the possibilities of the future.

Waiting and Silence

We are not the only artists. In fact, we aren't even the primary artists in the QUEST. God is. This is why waiting and silence are essential to this process. I have repeatedly used the word *emergence* to describe the process of discovering vision. Because this emergence originates with God, groups that ignore or avoid times of waiting and silence deny their need for the primary Artist.

> Groups that ignore or avoid times of waiting and silence deny their need for the primary Artist.

The reality is that emergence takes time. Not all things can be discerned—or solved, if you will—in one day or one meeting. Emergence grows in the soil of waiting. And waiting is something we struggle to embrace. Life and vision unfold at a pace that is slower than we are often comfortable with. This is one reason we must learn skill one, holding creative tension. Groups that wait in the QUEST allow space for God to orchestrate parts of the vision that are beyond their control.

Further, silence in the conversation is like a deep breath the group takes to remain connected to its Source. We live in a society that is uncomfortable with silence, especially in group settings. But constant noise lessens the substance of the conversation and the QUEST. There are times when a group pause is in order. Our propensity for noisemaking makes this a more difficult skill to integrate into the discussion. But it is critical that we do.

Because many groups are not skilled at silence and waiting, let me suggest ways to integrate these skills into your team.

Have a Brief Conversation About the Tools

One of the best ways to introduce these tools is simply to bring up the subject when the team is together. If you're the facilitator of the group, share your reasons for mentioning the topic. Ask participants what they think of the idea of integrating silence and waiting into the process. Do they share your desires? your fears? As a group, decide to pay attention to moments when silence and/or waiting would be appropriate, and seize those times when they arise.

Take Advantage of the Natural Rhythms of the Conversation

Dialogue tends to ebb and flow like ocean waves. There are moments in the conversation when the energy is intense and the people involved seem open and full of a kind of synergy that heightens the anticipation of the group. But, like a wave, those moments can't last forever. The wave must break. And when it does, groups will often intuitively want to pause. If the group is aware of the need for silence and waiting, this is a good time to simply suggest that the group wait in silence for a few moments. In other words, maximize what is occurring naturally.

This brief, intentional silence reminds people of the deeper purpose of the meeting and connects them more fully with the present moment. The next wave of conversation can then be fuller and freer because of this pause.

Waiting for More Than a Moment

Often a group will be unable to find a resolution to an issue in one meeting. Certain issues, usually those more weighty in nature, require time. When this is the case, it is best to "intentionalize" the waiting. That is, the group should consciously hold the creative tension outside of the meeting. I call this "thinkubating." Thinkubating is the process of active reflection during a time of group waiting. Simply put, the group decides to wait on purpose. Outside of the group meeting, participants are watching for God's hand and listening for his voice. It's amazing what can emerge outside the formal conversation when those involved are open to the subtle and not so subtle messages of God. The messages often come in the most unlikely times and places. The individual group members must keep their hearts attentive to these moments. Their role in this time of waiting is to thinkubate: to attend to the issue and watch for those messages. When the group reconvenes, take the time to share and examine these thinkubating moments.

Conversation Starters

- Do you find it hard to wait and/or to be silent in your personal life? If so, what exactly do you find challenging about waiting and silence?

- As a group or team, do you find it difficult to wait and/or to be silent?

- What dynamics specific to your team make waiting and silence difficult?

- Share a time you saw God orchestrate something for your team or group while you and your team waited in the tension.

{ EXPERIENCEercise }

INSTRUCTIONS: Practice group silence using this ancient spiritual practice. Sit in a circle with your team or group. Choose one person to watch the clock so that everyone else can relax and simply participate. Ask group members to choose a short phrase of Scripture to gently and silently turn over in their hearts and minds. Here's an example using Psalm 46:10: " 'Be still, and know that I am God.' We wait for you in silence."

Remain in a time of silent prayer for fifteen minutes.

Debriefing the EXPERIENCEercise

- How did the time of silence affect you as individuals?

- Did you find it awkward to "share" the silence as a group?

- What might change about your group or team if you practiced this regularly?

SKILL 3: PROVIDING FEEDBACK AND FEED FORWARD

The final process skill is that of feedback and feed forward. Feedback is a familiar concept, but it is worth revisiting here from the vantage point of group dynamics.

I have found in my work with groups—as well as my experience as a member of scores of groups—that group members find it difficult to give feedback to each other about process issues. Remember John, whom I mentioned early in this chapter? Because of John's behavior, his team developed "zones of undiscussable topics." What needed to occur with John and the team was a loving but candid conversation about their dysfunctional dance.

It's hard to have conversations about process, especially when they entail pointing out difficulties in relationships. Yet, without these loving, gentle, and firm conversations, groups will function only at shallow levels.

The pastoral staff I am a part of at North Way has served as a model for this kind of feedback. I am proud to serve on a team that cultivates honesty and transparency with care and intention. We certainly have a long way to go, but we have paid the price to get there. A few years ago, we determined to make our way through some "squishy spots" in our relationships. We had issues with one another, so we brought in a loving and wise facilitator who helped us navigate these areas. Some hard truth was spoken in love, and we all had to face ourselves as individuals and as part of a team.

Those early meetings opened the door for a deeper understanding of each other and a greater sense of unity and purpose. But it all began when we chose to take a risk and give each other feedback about issues that had hampered our relationships. We are now able to more freely give process feedback to each other when needed. The door is open. I would encourage you to be very thoughtful and sensitive when considering feedback of this sort. Though it has the potential for great benefit, it can also explode into a fireball of emotion and reaction. I would suggest you find a facilitator or consultant who understands how to navigate this terrain. If you're concerned that your group can't do this alone, don't! Get help.

I bumped into the concept of "feed forward" during my doctoral studies. Since that time, the concept has both intrigued and helped me. I first read about the idea in an article by Mary M. Crossan, Henry W. Lane, and Roderick E. White entitled "An Organizational Learning Framework: From Intuition to Institution." The authors describe it this way: "Feed forward relates to exploration. It is the transference of learning from individuals and groups...to the learning that becomes embedded—or institutionalized—in the form of systems, structures, strategies, and procedures."

The word I want to highlight in the quote above is *transference*. All communities need ways of transferring information from one team or individual to the entire group or community. Insights rarely emerge simultaneously across every level of a community. One group in the community, or one individual on the team, may serendipitously discover an important piece of vision or process. When this occurs, there must be a way to quickly transfer that learning to the whole. The individual or team must capture the learning so that it is not lost and so that it can be shared with the whole organism. Churches are notorious for losing important insights because they have no way to capture and catalog those insights.

Your team or community must find a way, as individuals and as a group, to remember what is discovered so that transference can occur. Without this, important insights and the wisdom hidden in them will be lost.

Conversation Starters

- Is it difficult for your team to give process and/or relational feedback? If not, what has allowed your team to move into this terrain? If so, what do you think keeps your team from this part of the conversation?

Warning: Remember my advice. If you feel your team is not ready to venture into these waters without a facilitator, stop and find someone who can help you take this important step.

CHAPTER 4

SABOTAGE POINT:
Poor Execution

Golf and the Conversation

I PLAYED A LOT OF GOLF AS A KID. When you grow up in Phoenix, it's a likely sport to learn because of the climate and the plethora of golf courses at your fingertips. Golf, like all sports, is about execution. Although you can learn a lot by listening to a coach or watching The Golf Channel, eventually you have to start swinging. It's at this point that the trouble begins. There are so many things that can go wrong once the club is in your hands: your stance, your weight distribution, the speed and trajectory of your swing, the position of your hands on the club, and on it goes.

My dad and I played a lot of golf together when I was growing up. When we played with someone else, he'd often watch the person's practice swing and then whisper to me, "The ball is going to go to the right," or "He's going to duff it," or "It's going to go straight up." Most of the time, my dad seemed prophetic—the ball would do exactly what he'd predicted. How did he know this? He knew because the way you execute your swing has direct consequences on where the ball travels and how it gets there. Golf is a game of execution. The same is true of dynamic discussions.

In the last chapter, we explored the importance of group communication to the conversation. The way groups implement communication skills will determine some of the direction their conversations are going to travel. In this chapter we'll examine another part of implementation that I will call *execution*. Execution has to do with the way the conversation is structured and employed. If a group misappropriates execution, it will sabotage the dialogue.

The most important thing to understand, with regard to execution, is that dynamic discussion can occur at any and every level of your church. Two people discussing the future of a ministry over lunch can experience an extremely creative and transformative moment. A team of pastors gathering to discuss specific issues can practice creative dialogue. Teams of people representing your entire church can consider large themes necessary for communitywide transformation. Teams of leaders and members who work in specific ministries can enter this kind of discussion.

Later in this chapter, I'll show you specific ways to execute creative conversation in your church regardless of its size and current structure. However, before I delve into these structures for execution, I'd like you to think briefly about a related issue: facilitation.

Facilitation

You need to think about facilitation before execution because if the conversation is facilitated poorly, it really doesn't matter how well you distribute the conversation; it will be over before it begins. My real fear in facilitation is the potential for leaders to automatically choose the role of facilitator and, in doing so, overfacilitate the conversation, thereby negating the collective and exploratory nature of the process. Let's consider a few facilitation blunders that leaders can easily make as facilitators.

"YOU'LL LIKE THIS...REALLY"

As I've already pointed out, too many leaders still believe it is their divine right and responsibility to discover and shape vision independent of the people. From this vantage point, members are simply the implementers of the great ideas of leaders. One of the worst examples of this is the pastor/leader who stands up in front of a group and conducts a monologue to sell the vision: "God's revealed the way to me, and now we must make it happen." Many pastors use inspirational language and their powers of persuasion to convince people, "You'll like this...really." Strong leadership language is used to convince and even cajole at times.

I believe this occurs because modern pastoral leaders read a modern leadership paradigm into Scripture. Leaders in the Bible had no models; they simply walked into the unknown one step at a time and discovered God and vision along the way with the people. The modern church's tendency to institutionalize everything has created a group of leaders who seriously think it is their mandate to tell everybody else what to do and how to do it—and even worse, do all this in the name of God.

"WHAT DO YOU MEAN, *WE* HELPED MAKE THE DECISION?"

Many leaders make another facilitation blunder when they carry on pseudo conversations. In this scenario, the pastor/leader understands that things go better when people "believe" they had a voice in the conversation—that whole "ownership thing." Therefore, in an attempt to seem like a consensus builder, the pastor draws people into the conversation, creating the feeling that the group is helping to make a decision about an important issue. However, all the while he or she already knows the end point; the decisions have already been made. The conversation is for show—for "ownership."

The really lamentable aspect of this scenario is that when things fall apart—which often happens—the pastor/leader has the nerve to blame the people or other leaders for the mess of the moment, crying, "Hey, you helped get us here!"

"WHATEVER YOU WANT—YOU PAY THE BILLS"

Of course equally disturbing is the spineless pastor/leader who doesn't understand that part of leadership is to challenge the ideas of the people so that the people and the ideas become whole and healthy. A pastor driven by fear or the almighty dollar has no vision but the vision of those who whine the loudest or contribute the most.

Conversation Starters

- Which of the facilitation blunders are you most prone to? Why? What does this reveal about your personality and leadership style?

EXPERIENCEercise

If you are going to facilitate a dynamic discussion, invite a trusted friend to attend the meeting. After the discussion, ask your friend to share constructive feedback that will help you grow as a facilitator. Ask him or her to be brutally honest.

You may also want to solicit the feedback of a member of the group whom you don't know. This will give you a different kind of objective feedback. Facilitation is an art that is learned through reflective practice. This kind of feedback is critical to a facilitator's growth.

GOOD ADVICE ABOUT GOOD FACILITATION

Whether you're a pastor or not, if you're facilitating the conversation, here are some important ingredients you'll need for the journey. First, good facilitators describe the topic as clearly as possible and then let others round out the description until there is a group understanding about it. Even though pockets of ambiguity will surface, beginning with clarity about the topic enables members of the group to harness their energy and move in the same direction. I've seen numerous conversations unravel simply because the topic at hand was unclear.

Second, good facilitators know how to steward the QUEST. They understand the importance of the QUEST and leave space for each aspect. Good facilitators are not threatened by the ambiguity, frustration, and challenge of the QUEST. Because of this, they can help the group find the patterns and themes in the conversation. They also have a sense of when it's time to narrow the conversation and move from ambiguity to clarity. In fact, they know how to ebb and flow around ambiguity and clarity. Wise facilitators understand that the art of conversation is not only about the moment of the conversation, but the incarnation of the vision as it emerges. They help steward the energy of the group toward that aim. This can be done even if the facilitator holds no formal position of leadership in the group.

Finally, and perhaps most important, good facilitators understand that there will be many moments in the conversation in which they must allow others to facilitate. Perhaps the greatest skill of a facilitator is learning to let go of the reins of facilitation by allowing another to do all the things I've mentioned above.

Structures for Execution

I know the next several pages will leave you with questions and concerns. I've addressed

---

{ **Conversation Starters**

- Which aspects of the advice I've given to facilitators do you practice most naturally? (This is a bright spot.)

- Which aspect of the advice I've suggested do you have the hardest time implementing? (It's a blind spot.)

Keep these bright and blind spots in mind as you facilitate. Don't sleepwalk your way through the process. Stay alert and sensitive to your strengths and weaknesses.

---

some of those concerns at the end of the chapter. For now, let's look at viable ways to instigate dynamic dialogue throughout your community.

STRUCTURE 1: THE HOURGLASS

The hourglass method is built on expansion, contraction, and re-expansion. This method of execution can work at any level of your community, but it's particularly helpful when you want to invite a sample of the entire community into a conversation. In this conversational structure, a group that represents the entire church gathers for the first round of conversations. Perhaps your church is considering the purchase of land. This is a big decision that requires dynamic dialogue and genuine ownership. The hourglass method enables you to sample a large segment of your population in a relatively short amount of time and explore whether the land under consideration (or whatever issue you face) is indeed part of your emerging vision.

An hourglass is widest on the ends and narrow in the middle. The hourglass represents the shape of the distribution of the conversation. Conversation 1 represents a broad segment of your church; Conversation 2 narrows the conversation to senior leadership; and Conversation 3 re-opens the discussion to a segment of your total church population.

Conversation 1

You can determine the number of people in Conversation 1 a number of ways. Here are two ideas.

The small sample includes no more than twelve people. Because of the way the hourglass conversation unfolds, you don't want many of your senior staff leaders to participate in this first conversation if you choose the small sample. The senior pastor and one other staff representative will do just fine.

The large sample may include as many as two hundred people. This group represents the same diversity as the small sample; the only difference is the larger number of participants. If you go with the large sample for the first conversation, you'll want to form groups of ten to twelve for the conversation itself. In this case, you may want senior staff to facilitate each group. In other words, the two hundred won't converse together; rather, they'll converse in small groups and then report back to the whole. One facilitator will keep the large group on track and move it between large- and small-group conversations.

Whether you chose the small or large sample for Conversation 1 of the hourglass conversation, the goals are the same: to find the common pool of meaning and to discover the emerging vision together.

Each group will journal its conversation so that important ideas are not lost throughout the day. Participants in this first part of the hourglass conversation understand that they are *not* making decisions at this point; they're exploring the terrain.

Conversation 2

The ideas generated during Conversation 1 are then taken to the senior leadership team for Conversation 2. You will have to determine who represents the senior leadership of your church. In a larger church, this is often a group of pastors who have been charged with the responsibility of daily oversight of the ministry. In some denominational churches, this is the session or presbytery. The second part of the hourglass method narrows the group to the people who make up this senior leadership body.

At the beginning of Conversation 2, the insights from Conversation 1 are briefly shared. If members of senior leadership desire, they may invite one or two people from Conversation 1 to join them in this conversation. On the other hand, the senior leaders may discern that it's important for them to dialogue without others present.

The senior leadership then carries on the QUEST in a more focused way. Because the leaders have a perspective that the people in the first conversation don't have, they can further shape the information gathered. The viewpoints of the participants in Conversation 1 are critical, but so are the views of the leaders.

I encourage the leaders in Conversation 2 to restrain themselves from reaching a conclusion. Decision is not yet necessary; discernment of the emerging vision is what matters most. This does not mean that decisions should be forever avoided. Nor does it mean that leaders shouldn't have a major role in making the decision. However, leaders must be aware of their propensity to hurry a process due to their impatience. I've seen leaders—in the name of urgency for the vision—make all kinds of rash and poor decisions. Actually, I've done it myself. If leaders (and members, for that matter) allow God and the emergent process the necessary space, clarity has a way of surfacing.

Conversation 3

The third piece of the hourglass conversation unites groups 1 and 2 for a third conversation. The facilitator begins by sharing the history of the conversation—what occurred in Conversations 1 and 2. Issues that surfaced in the senior leadership conversation are shared with the group unless it is not appropriate to do so for reasons of sensitivity.

However, these sensitive areas should be few and far between—the more open the sharing, the better. In between Conversations 2 and 3, the facilitator or the senior leadership will have narrowed the topics. The goal of this third session is still not to arrive at a decision, but rather to obtain the best collective wisdom of the group. Conversation 3 also serves to further unite leaders and members around the emerging vision. Remember, it is the collective wisdom of the group that is the aim of the conversation.

As I mentioned earlier, the hourglass method works best in addressing major issues facing a church. Don't expend the energy necessary to pull this kind of conversation together to discuss what type of soap dispensers work best. Rather, use this method to reach major church decisions that require the collective wisdom of your community. But bear in mind that the method can be used at any level. If the children's ministry leaders want to delve into their overall strategy for scope and sequence learning issues, they could use the hourglass method to do so.

STRUCTURE 2: THE SMALL GROUP/ SUNDAY SCHOOL METHOD

Another way to engage large groups of people in dynamic discussion is by utilizing your church's already existing structures. Most churches already have ways to move people into smaller groups for growth and community. These may be Sunday school classes, small groups, or ministry groups. For church leaders who are seeking input on definitive issues and want to connect a large segment of their community to the conversation, these groups are natural places to carry on the dialogue.

A Brief Video and Facilitation Guide

To begin the discovery process using this method, have the leadership team create a short video explaining the situation. Videos are now easy to make, fairly inexpensive to produce, and simple to distribute. Along with the video, provide the leaders of these groups with a crash course in facilitating dynamic dialogue. Don't get bogged down here. The goal is not to send these leaders through intensive training. Simply give them the basics of facilitation, and let them go.

Ask groups to journal their QUEST as the conversation unfolds, creating a set of questions and helpful comments as they surface. After they return these journals, compile and codify them into patterns and themes. If this process is not stewarded correctly, you will have an informational nightmare on your hands. The larger the group structure, the greater the possible nightmare. To circumvent the nightmare, you must make it clear that you want groups to QUEST, and then refine their QUEST to one or two priorities. Ask each group to summarize its QUEST experience by identifying the one most glaring blind spot and the greatest bright spot it discovered concerning the issue at hand. This enables someone to codify all of the information much more quickly.

After discovering patterns and themes during the first round of conversation, you could produce another video describing the information that surfaced in this first round and then focus the groups on a narrower QUEST for the next round. The iterations necessary for this type of conversational structure must be discerned along the way. There will be times where one conversation is plenty to glean what's needed. However, at other times, a second or third round may help refine the vision and unite the community.

STRUCTURE 3: TEAM-BY-TEAM MINISTRY

Many churches organize around ministry teams. These teams represent the main areas in the community in which energy is released to fulfill vision. Using these teams is another natural way to distribute the conversation. In this method, ministry leaders come together for an initial briefing on the conversation at hand. They bring initial clarity to the conversation and are given the basics on the art of conversation. Each team leader then goes to the team he or she serves and conducts a round of conversations with those people.

After the teams have met, the leaders return to share their conversations and narrow the bandwidth for the next round—if another round is deemed necessary. The rounds can continue until there is a sense of collective vision and wisdom.

{ Conversation Starters

- After examining the conversational methods in this chapter, which one(s) do you think would work in your community?

- What issues are you currently facing that would benefit from the kind of intentional conversations outlined in this chapter? What would it take to organize the conversation? What's holding you back?

Be Flexible

I want to be quick to point out that these methods for distributing the conversation are *possible* pathways for you to use. I encourage you to craft your own method of distribution based on what you know about your community.

One of these methods may work just fine for your situation. But it may be that crafting your own or forming a hybrid will better suit your specific community. Don't get too bogged down in designing the method, though. It will likely morph along the way. Also remember that these structures will work in micro and macro settings. They can work for one team as well as the entire community. Simply adjust the structure to fit the size and needs of the group engaged in the dialogue.

Concerns, Objections, and Questions

This section on execution may have raised some objections and questions in your mind. Now I'll address some of these objections and continue to clarify what this conversation can become in your community.

TIME, TIME, TIME

"Are you kidding? How much time do you think we have, anyway?" As you read the possible scenarios for the conversation, you might have smiled, laughed, and wondered what planet I was on when I wrote this chapter.

The first way I would respond to this objection is with an equation of sorts: *When it comes to dynamic discussion, the level of distribution should equal the magnitude of the topic.* If your church is considering a complete campus relocation or an entire overhaul of your ministry strategy, the conversation should be widespread. At times like these, it's worth the investment to engage a significant portion of your community in the dialogue.

If your church is deciding on the spiritual-formation strategy of its student ministries, the same magnitude of distribution may not be required. Although a fairly large group of people could still be involved in the conversation, the issue probably wouldn't rise to the magnitude of an issue like campus relocation. This has nothing to do with its importance; it's about the scope of its effects on the community. It's up to you and senior leadership to decide which matters require the involvement of the entire community.

I would also remind leaders who believe this would be a waste of time that I am suggesting a different mental model by which to discover vision. People in the church need to be engaged in the conversation at whatever level is deemed possible. And the "in-a-hurry" leader must be willing to appropriately slow down the process long enough to include them. Here comes another equation: *The pace of the conversation should reflect the magnitude of the issue.* A decision about a campus relocation should take longer than one week and should include many wise voices. Planning the next training seminar for small-group leaders could occur in one meeting of a few people. Either way, including people in the conversation will always slows things down, and that's appropriate.

THIS ALL SEEMS SO CONTRIVED

You may find the methods I've suggested cold and sterile. They may seem like nothing more than manipulative techniques that miss the very heart of what I've been describing as dynamic dialogue. "Maybe it would be better to simply let these conversations stay spontaneous and not program them," you might think.

As I hope you can tell by now, I'm not a big program guy. However, the reality remains that if you want to engage a significant number of people in the conversation, you're going to need a structure by which to do it—unless you want the process to take five years.

I would also add that the sterility of the distribution lies more in the way it's stewarded than in its logistics. If you make the process warm and inviting, it will be just that. If it's nothing more than a calculated way to get people on board or quell their objections, you've missed the point anyway.

WHO GETS TO MAKE THE CALL AT THE END
OF THE CONVERSATION?

After reading the methods I've described, you may be wondering if I'm calling for a radically democratic process for all decision making. You might believe that this kind of conversation would cause people to believe they get to make every decision the church faces, which could paralyze the ministry.

To deal with this objection, I would first simply refer to the title of the book. This entire concept is about inviting your community into dynamic *dialogue*. The title is not *Dynamic Decisions*. I'm not suggesting that everyone should vote on definitive decisions facing your community. I realize that church government comes into play here, and I'm sensitive to the fact that the decision-making process is different for every church. However, just as size doesn't matter in the conversation, neither does church government. This is because the conversation is not initiated to make the decision, but to find the collective wisdom and vision emerging in the community.

Decision-making bodies will actually find their roles strengthened and supported by listening to the wisdom that comes from the group.

If the decision is theirs to make, then they need to make the final decision. Dynamic dialogue only enables a better decision.

THIS WILL BREED MORE TROUBLE THAN IT'S WORTH

You may be thinking, "In a perfect world, maybe, but this idea opens the door for too much complaining and disagreement." You may be envisioning conversations breaking out all over your church— breaking out like a virus. You might be thinking that if we all lived in Eden, these ideas might have a chance, but since that's not the case, this is a big mistake.

It's important to allow for some disagreement in the conversation. As we've already seen, ambiguity and chaos are not the enemies of innovative communication. In fact, initial disagreement is often necessary for the conversation to flourish. Quashing disagreement, especially early on, can lead to manipulative monologues and forced chatting that lead nowhere fast. Plus, whether you want to hear it or not, disagreement exists.

Disagreement is part of the QUEST. But remember, people need to be schooled in the basics of dynamic discussion. One of those basics is the idea of group sculpting. Our individual opinions are important, but they must ultimately surrender to the collective wisdom we are seeking. Of course, certain people do want to stir up trouble and can throw a wrench in the process. However, don't let the conversation be dictated by those few troublemakers. They're going to do their thing regardless of what you do. So deal with them and move on.

If people understand that they're not in the conversation to make the decision but to help find collective wisdom and vision, they are often more willing to lay down their views for *the* view. In other words, if they realize that they're influencing the process but not making the decision, they're in a better position to discern and disclose helpful insights.

QUICK AGREEMENT: WATCH OUT FOR "FEEL GOOD" RESULTS

One danger to watch for in the process is quick agreement. If things go too smoothly, you've probably not conversed long enough or honestly enough. Quick agreement is usually a signal that one viewpoint is being forced or that people are fearful of speaking their hearts and minds. Good facilitators, sensing quick agreement, may need to throw the group into good chaos by introducing concerns that are not being vocalized.

IS EVERY VOICE HEARD EQUALLY?

My initial answer here is yes *and* no. Of course from one vantage point, the playing field is level throughout the conversation. We honor everyone's voice and view. Without this appreciation, the conversation is contrived from the get-go. If people don't feel honored in the conversation—heard—they will shut down, and monologues will abound. True and deep listening is part of the honoring process.

Of course, there are going to be voices that sound louder in the conversation. This is not necessarily a problem. In fact, it is a necessary part of the conversation. Leaders do have a unique viewpoint, and their responsibility for stewarding vision does create distinctiveness to their voice and volume. But this distinctiveness must be tempered by other voices. For instance, there may be someone in the conversation who brings an inordinate amount of wisdom to the table but little positional power. This voice must be heard if the true goal is collective wisdom.

WHAT ABOUT LEADERSHIP?

You may be thinking I am just against leadership—maybe I have an ax to grind. This is certainly not the case. I've spent way too much money, time, and energy pursuing a doctorate in organizational leadership. I've been a positional leader in the church for almost twenty years. I'm not throwing stones at something I know nothing about or have no passion to pursue. Dynamic dialogue is not meant to be an anti-leadership approach to ministry. Rather, it's a call to rethink the shape of leadership in the decades ahead as leaders become deft at facilitating the conversation and discovering the vision.

Conversation Starters

- Of all these questions and objections, which one best describes your concerns?

- Do you have a concern I didn't mention? What would it take to overcome that concern?

CHAPTER 5

CONVERSING ABOUT MISSION: How Can You Discover Your Church's Emerging Mission?

WHEN I WAS A FRESHMAN in high school, I fell into a little hero worship of a senior named Steve. To me, Steve pretty much walked on water—he could do no wrong. He became an icon of coolness to a short ninth-grader who could only hope to someday be in a similar ZIP code of cool. Steve exuded confidence. He was popular. He was a musician, excelled in academics, and dated pretty much whomever he wanted... you've got the picture.

As an impressionable freshman, I was looking for role models. Steve was number one on my list. Over time, I was bold enough to actually strike up a conversation with Steve, and he actually seemed to like me. We became casual friends. As I hung out with Steve, I found myself trying hard to be like him. There was just one problem: I wasn't Steve.

Steve had wavy hair that fell in tiny, circular wisps all over his head. My hair was as straight as the street I grew up on, and when freshly cut, it stuck straight out of my head. Steve was lean and about five feet, eleven inches tall. My freshman year, the Christian singer Evie was popular. She sang a song with these words: "I'm only four feet eleven, but I'm going to heaven." Let's just say, that was my theme song. I was a short, slightly overweight runt—if you can imagine that combination!

I could go on, but you get the idea. As a freshman it was so hard to be OK with myself because...well, there was Steve. He was a living reminder of everything I wanted to be. Because of my desire to be like Steve, it became hard to find my own life, my own gifts, my own self. This icon overshadowed me, and for a season I gave up on my own life to pursue his. Luckily for me, he graduated, which forced me to continue my own growth.

My adolescent obsession with cool Steve reminds me of what I see occurring in a lot of churches these days. Pastors and other leaders of small, medium, and large churches flock to the most successful churches in the land. These are the cool churches. These are the churches that have achieved the size and stature that the pastors and leaders of smaller churches dream of achieving. Pastors and leaders sit around wishing they could be more like these churches. Or they adopt the cool churches' methodology—lock, stock, and barrel—hoping that will do the trick. There's only one problem: It's impossible to become one of these cool churches, because every church must become itself.

Now don't get me wrong. Steve was a very good influence in my life. Through his own example, he caused me to aspire to do my best academically and musically. But for a while, it was hard to tell me apart from Steve. I became a little clone. Steve didn't mean for this to happen. In fact, he probably had no idea that it did. Nevertheless it did occur, and I was more interested in being Steve than being Dave.

> The basic mission of each church is to become a truly unique expression of Jesus.

The cool churches I'm referring to are indeed good churches. I have no ax to grind with any of them. Well, OK maybe one—but it's a little ax. I believe that these churches have inadvertently made it too alluring to be like them. I mean, really. Have you been to a cool church's conference? It's rather overwhelming. Even if the leaders of the cool church beg people not to take their models back and simply implement them (as if they're ready-to-assemble kits), leaders often do just that. The temptation to try to become even one-tenth like the cool church is hard to resist. Do we really need clones of cool churches, or do we need every church to be its own original cool?

"But Dave, aren't these churches providing valuable resources that most churches in America could not produce even if they tried?" you might question. "And," you continue, "why should every church reinvent the wheel? Can't we learn from the cool churches' experiences and use them to further our own work?" My answer to those questions is a qualified yes. Certainly these cool churches do have resources that can and should be shared. And churches don't have to reinvent every wheel. But there is one wheel your church must not adopt from another, and that is the wheel of its emerging mission.

I'm uncomfortable when a church implements the mission of another church without doing the hard work of QUESTing after its own vision and mission. To simply adopt what has emerged somewhere else is to forgo the power of the search. Further, it does not create a band of QUESTers who will, in the long run, continue to explore and discover their own unique purpose.

My dream is to create a national pastors' conference that touts no cool church model. Instead, pastors learn the skill of dynamic dialogue, and, more to the point of this chapter, they learn how to discover their own cool and emerging mission. For now, this chapter will have to do.

Why Can't You Be a "Cool Church's" Clone?

What's so wrong with being a cool church's clone anyway? Aren't God's principles universal? Don't they work anywhere and everywhere? Yes, certain principles are timeless. But the gospel is to be contextualized in your community in ways it cannot be contextualized in others. It's not possible for your church to become the cool church's clone because it exists in a different spot on the space-time continuum in our society. You face unique people and situations that require your church itself to be unique.

With all this in mind, let me define *mission* this way: Mission is the localization of timeless truth. You could argue that every church has the same basic mission, and I know this is often what the cool churches try to help us recognize. But I disagree with this notion. The basic mission of each church is to become a truly unique expression of Jesus. We don't all have to be the same or do all the same things!

All of this comes down to incarnation. Your church must incarnate the kingdom in a unique and powerful way. I want to encourage you to pay the price of QUESTing after that unique incarnation. Learn from the cool churches how they QUEST. But don't take their QUEST and make it your own.

Conversation Starters

- Do you agree that too many churches copy the ways of the cool churches? Why do you think this happens?

- Have you noticed this propensity to copy in your own community? In what ways has this tendency hurt your church?

Mission: First Identity, Then Activity

The reason many churches adopt the missions of cool churches stems from our current view and definition of *mission*. Mission is primarily seen as the activity we generate in order to fulfill the vision we desire. And to some degree, that is a good description. However, it is only one side of the mission coin. The other side invites us to discover our communal identity. In fact, it might be better to say that *identity* should occur just a little ahead of *activity* in the pursuit of mission.

When people seek their missions in life, many considerations become part of their QUESTs. They ask, "How has my history shaped me? Why did I grow up in the family I grew up in? What have my experiences taught me? What gifts do I possess? Where is the voice of God in all of this? What is this current moment asking of me?" And on it goes. These and other questions help to shape a person's calling at any given moment. As we go through life, we ask these questions again and again and learn more about ourselves. Through it all we become the originals we were meant to be.

All of this QUESTing converges in time and space to become our current mission. As I write this book, I realize it would take another book to describe all the dynamics that led to this moment in my life. This moment of personal *mission expression* is the culmination of so many other mission moments I've experienced. And, Lord willing, this moment will become the soil for many more.

This process occurs not only in individuals, but also in communities. The parallels between our individual and collective callings are striking. Communities were meant to discover their unique callings through the leading of the Spirit and the QUEST found in dynamic dialogue. A cool church can certainly assist another church in its QUEST, *but it cannot replace or become the focus of that QUEST.*

> First, determine who you are; second, determine what you do.

Communal mission, then, is the exploration of your church's unique identity and the discovery of how, through that identity, God is calling you to achieve specific goals. The order is this: First, determine who you are; second, determine what you do. The remainder of this chapter will guide you and your team or community in exploring your identity and the related activity that makes up your mission. (We'll look even more deeply at *activity* in Chapters 6 and 7.)

QUESTing to Your Mission Identity
DISCOVERING AND HONORING
YOUR ACTIONSPACE

One of the first elements important to the discovery of mission identity and activity is "actionspace." Actionspace is the local field your community has been planted in, from which you incarnate your mission. Your actionspace is the place from which you contextualize your mission—making it the original it was meant to be. Understanding the community around your church, and the one inside your walls, is critical to your mission identity. This is a bit different from simply understanding the demographics of your area or creating a profile of the typical person in your community. Understanding your actionspace helps you understand *who you are* and *who you need to become*. Your community's actionspace is composed of the situations and relationships around you. These relationships and situations matter beyond measure and help you discover your mission's identity and activity.

PEOPLE, PEOPLE, PEOPLE

The people in your actionspace are as critical to your identity as they are to your activity. Churches tend to focus on what the people in the actionspace can *do* for the mission. But before you consider what they can do, you need to understand who those people are. *Their individual identities will help you discover your communal one.*

My favorite visual reminder of this concept is composite photography. (See page 76 for an example.) In this type of photography, many little pictures combine to make up one larger one. From a distance you see the larger picture. But, as you move closer, you discover that the larger picture is made up of hundreds of individual pictures. Each individual picture helps to form the larger picture, but the most important picture is the one all the little pictures make together. Perfect! This is exactly how people (within and without) help to form the mission identity of your actionspace.

People Who Think of Your Church as Home

Let's begin with the people (pictures) who call your church "home." These are people who not only attend regularly, but who also participate significantly in the life of your church community. Begin by asking the following questions.

• Who are these people? How would you describe them?

• If you had to describe their concerns, what words would you use?

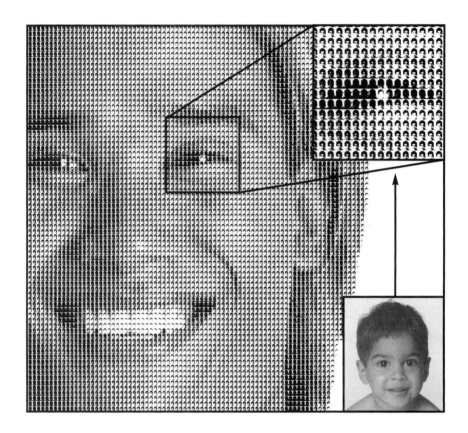

- Why do you think they were drawn to your church, and why have they stayed?

- If you had to describe their passions, what words would you use?

- How are these people viewed in your larger community/city?

- How are these people similar to the leaders of your church? How are they different?

- What activities of your church seem to energize these people, and what deflates them? What does the answer to this question tell you about them and the activity that's important to them?

{ EXPERIENCEercise }

SUPPLIES: a white board or large sheet of newsprint and markers

INSTRUCTIONS: Based on your answers to the questions on page 76, write on a white board or large sheet of newsprint fifty single words that describe this group of people. Do this quickly; don't think too much (it hurts anyway). After completing this, eliminate the words that seem repetitive. Then narrow the remaining words to the five most definitive and important words on the list. Finally, put those five words into one sentence that begins, "The people who regularly attend and significantly participate in our community are..."

OPTIONAL

Ask the questions on page 76 of five people in your church who attend and participate in your church. Discuss with them how their identities shape your church's identity. See if they agree or had ever thought of it this way. Ask them to describe how they might view the church differently if they believed the individuals within the community helped to shape its mission. (I think you'll be surprised by how intriguing and energizing the conversation will become!)

People Who Rarely or Never Think of Your Church

The second group of people who help to shape your mission's identity and activity are those people in the immediate community around your church. These people rarely or never attend your church but are part of your community or city. These are neighbors who live or work near your church, and they are also in some way connected to the people who call your church home. They can be neighbors, co-workers, and friends.

We don't usually think of this second group of people as shaping the identity of our actionspace, but in fact they do. This group and the group that calls your church "home" live in the same city and experience the same local culture. Both groups do "life" together, even if it is only as acquaintances. These groups are concerned about the same schools, local political issues, and regional events. Together they endure the local weather and other events that directly affect their daily lives.

As I said, those inside and outside your actionspace experience the same culture, but it's really more than that. They form that culture as they experience it. If you've lived in more than one city, you know what I mean by this. People in various regions of the country have different cultural expressions because of the way they see and do life. And much of this cultural uniqueness dates back generations.

North Way, the church I currently serve, is located just outside of Pittsburgh, Pennsylvania. After arriving, my wife and I quickly discovered the differences between the culture of Pittsburgh and that of Tucson or Phoenix, Arizona, where we grew up. We've also lived in Maryland and Denver and found those local cultures different as well.

One of the first things I noticed about Pittsburgh was just how unusual North Way is to the local community. It's an anomaly of sorts to those who live in the North Hills. North Way is a nondenominational church of around three thousand. To many Pittsburghers, North Way is barely considered a church. First, it's way too big to be a church. Churches in Pittsburgh are small and located in neighborhoods. We look like nothing else in the area. In Phoenix, there are North Ways on nearly every corner of the city. Large churches are simply part of the culture. Not so in Pittsburgh.

In addition, we are frequently asked, "How can you be a church and not be connected to a denomination?" Pittsburgh is, and always has been, a very traditional area in that people know their roots. "I'm Irish Catholic (or Italian Catholic or Lutheran or Presbyterian). What are you guys?" goes the question. In the western United States, people seem to care less about clustering around ethnicity—not that it doesn't happen, but it's not as prevalent. A generation ago, people in Pittsburgh lived in clusters according to their race and creed. The West was (and still is) a melting pot. Now this is changing, even in Pittsburgh. But the mentality is not gone.

North Way's actionspace is very different from the actionspace of a church in Phoenix. The people in the actionspace are different; they have different roots and different concerns. Of course, there are national and global concerns that bind us all together, but the people nearest you who are not in your church play a part in shaping your identity. Do you know them? Do you understand them?

Conversation Starters

- How would you describe this second group of people?

- What are their concerns, hopes, and dreams?

- How do you think they view your church? What are the reasons behind these views, from your vantage point?

SUPPLIES: a white board or large sheet of newsprint and markers

INSTRUCTIONS: Based on your answers to the questions on page 76, write on a white board or large sheet of newsprint fifty single words that describe the people in your community who rarely or never think of your church. Do this quickly; don't think too much. After completing this, eliminate the words that seem repetitive. Then narrow the remaining words to the five most definitive and important words on the list. Finally, put those five words into one sentence that begins, "The people in our community who do not regularly attend our church and participate significantly in it are..."

OPTIONAL
Take five people from your community to lunch. Tell them you want to hear about their lives and concerns. Assure them that you want nothing from them, nor are you trying to get them to attend your church. You just want to listen to determine how your church is perceived in the community and how it can help the community. Then listen! Get to know them as people so you can later reflect on what they teach you about your mission's identity.

SITUATIONAL MATTERS

Another vital component to the identity and activity of your action-space is the situational milieu of your church and the larger community. What kinds of situations are pressing on your church these days? What about your larger community or city—what issues are pressing on it? Situations matter because they reveal what is shaping the cultures (your church's and the larger community's) and how the cultures are pushing back.

Situational Matters in Your Church

It's important to remember that the situational matters that help identify your church's mission are highly fluid and dynamic. Imagine a balloon about two-thirds full of water. If you press on the balloon, you will alter its shape. On one level the balloon's identity remains the same; it's still a balloon. However, at another very real level, its identity is re-formed again and again by the changing pressure of your hand. This is how situations will alter the identity and activity of your church's actionspace. They press on parts of the actionspace, or all of it, in specific ways. This pressing changes the shape of the space and requires your church's identity and activity to morph (sometimes very quickly) as well.

It's important to look at these *situational pressings* through wide as well as zoom lenses. Certain broad situations shape the entire church and are shaped by it. This is the wide-angle look and includes situations such as the purchasing of land, relocation, overall strategy initiatives, and worship styles. These situations create pressure—healthy and otherwise—on the culture of your actionspace. Moreover, they begin to define your church's identity. It's easy to see this in connection with your church's worship style, which becomes an identifying marker for people both inside and outside of your church. Changing that worship style sends a message that you are changing the church's identity.

Zoom-angle situations occur in localized areas of your church such as the student ministries or worship ministries. For example, your small-group ministries may be in a time of significant leadership transition. This will definitely alter at least that part of your actionspace. Further,

Conversation Starters

- Are these situations viewed by the church community as mainly positive or mainly negative?

- How are these wide-angle situations pressing on the church?

- How is this *pressing* changing the identity of your church? In other words, what are these situations requiring of you and your actionspace?

- Can you identify a localized situation that is affecting your church's entire actionspace? Is there a particular ministry or team that is pressing on the whole? What is this doing to your actionspace?

- What situations inside your church are pressing on its entire actionspace?

localized situations can affect the entire church community. A moral failure of a leader is a localized situation, but the effects will be far-reaching. Tension in one area of ministry—children's ministry, for example—can ripple through the entire actionspace.

Situational Matters Beyond Your Church

Just as the people outside your church help to shape its mission, so situations outside your church press on its actionspace, requiring it to reshape its identity and activity. In the days following 9/11, for example, North Way and the police and firefighting communities bonded more significantly than at any other time in the church's history. The situation itself and the memorials that followed brought the two groups together in new ways and gave each group a greater appreciation for the other. Because of our response and collaboration with those groups during those days, our identity changed in their eyes. We were no longer the big church with lots of traffic, but a partner in cultivating a community of peace. This identity change would not have occurred if the church hadn't discerned the situation and entered into it with intention and grace.

Countless situations outside the walls of your church can press on the shape of its actionspace. Some will be rather insignificant, but others will dramatically alter your church's identity and activity. Those in the actionspace must pay attention to these situational pressings and determine *through creative dialogue* when to press back and respond in some manner. This fluid movement, over time, will continually reshape your church's identity and activity with regard to the larger community. Does this help you see just how emergent mission can be?

Conversation Starters

- Share a situation outside your church that reshaped its actionspace identity and activity.

- What enabled your church to respond to that situation? Did the situation increase your church's credibility in the community at large? If so, how?

- What current situations in the community are pressing on your mission's identity and activity?

- Do any of these situations call for a greater response from your church?

MORE MISSION CONSIDERATIONS

People and situations are the primary shapers of your mission's identity and activity. However, there are other forces at work in the actionspace that are worth noting.

Historical Threads

Your church's history is not simply "behind you." It's part of you. Each church needs to have a good grasp of its history. I don't mean to suggest that a church must remain locked in the ways of the past, but rather that the past holds an important message about the future of the church's mission.

Certain characteristics are woven into a church at its inception and during its early formative years. I call these *historical threads*. Historical threads are unique qualities of a church that seem to endure in the midst of every transition the church makes. At North Way, for instance, worship has a unique place in the church's life. It's not more important than other ministries, but it has a different texture. It's always evident regardless of the season, the transition, or the style.

From day one, the church's worship ministry drew people to the church for an authentic experience of God. People are touched at the core in unexplainable ways during the worship experience—not only because it's done with great passion and skill, but also because of an indefinable, intangible "something" that transcends human effort. It is simply how God moves in this particular church. I'm not trying to suggest that North Way is better than other churches. Rather, my point is that God has put a unique fingerprint on North Way that is manifested through corporate worship. I visit many other churches, and I haven't found that same fingerprint. However, I do find other fingerprints that reveal the historical threads at work in those communities—spiritual formation, a genuine ministry to the poor, mentoring ministries, and counseling ministries, for example.

I'm not suggesting that each church must find one ministry to emphasize above all others. Let me say it again: Historical threads are not more important than other ministries. However, these threads do tell you something important about your actionspace and how God works uniquely within it.

Historical threads are important to discover and sustain. It's not about keeping a "pet ministry" alive beyond its usefulness. It's about sustaining a directive that seems to transcend the dynamic fluctuations of mission that I spoke of earlier. The thread is a unique part of the church's DNA. It's like the little extra piece of cartilage at the end of my nose that makes my nose round. No matter how my body changes, this part of my nose comes along through every change. It's a thread that defines me as me (not one I'm crazy about, but...).

Conversation Starters }

- Can you identify a historical thread in your church? (If the church has one, it shouldn't be hard to identify.)
- How has this thread shaped your mission's identity and activity over the years? What does this thread tell you about your church's unique vision?

Beliefs, Philosophies, and Convictions

We don't all view the world the same way. We may share certain common principles and ideas, but we also craft a view of the world that is unique to us. This is as true of churches as it is of individuals. Churches do form a kind of shared reality. The unique expressions of faith communities are the result, in part, of this constructed reality. Theology and overall ministry philosophy will shape your mission's identity. For instance, though I've never been to either church, I can guarantee you that Cedar Ridge Community Church (where Brian McLaren is senior pastor) and Grace Community Church (where John MacArthur is senior pastor) have different mission identities based on their theologies and ministry philosophies. I'm not trying to elevate one of these identities over another. Nor am I suggesting that the identity is solely due to the senior leader of either church. But I do believe that the mission identities of the two churches are different based on their constructed realities of theology, belief, and ministry philosophy.

It's All About *Now*

Perhaps the entire exploration of mission is wrapped up in the present moment. It is the total gestalt of the past, present, and future. It is everything we have been, are, and hope to be, expressed in the *now*. Dynamic dialogue opens the church to the present moment and enables that community to discern its identity. From that discovery, meaningful ministry activity can emerge.

Conversation Starters

- How do you think your church's theology shapes its mission's identity and activity?

- Give specific examples of how these beliefs shape the actionspace.

- Are you satisfied with the interplay between your theology and philosophy and the identity those views portray to those inside and outside your community?

CHAPTER **6**

CONVERSING ABOUT MINISTRY:
How Can You Determine the Effectiveness of Your Church's Activities?

Dance With Me

SEVERAL YEARS AGO my wife forced—I mean *asked*—me to take dancing lessons with her. She'd been interested in swing dancing for some time and discovered that a group was forming to learn a related dance known as the Lindy Hop. She excitedly explained that there was still space in the class and that a couple of our friends had already signed up. "Oh, joy," I thought.

Before our first lesson began, thirty or so of us gathered in a circle and met Ben, the instructor. Ben reminded me of a sleek male mannequin with every hair in place. He had a lean body and fluid movements sure to "wow" women of all ages. From that moment on, I didn't like Ben.

Of course, there was nothing wrong with Ben or his female counterparts who taught the class. I was the one with the problem. I grew up watching old Fred Astaire movies. To me, Fred was poetry in motion. As a kid, I was captivated by his moves and dreamed of becoming a suave dancer who, with one look or move, could mesmerize and thrill women. Suffice it to say, things didn't work out that way.

Ben actually reminded me of Fred, so I couldn't figure out why I disliked him. But eventually, it dawned on me. To me, Fred Astaire was nothing more than an icon on the screen. I could dance vicariously through him. I could "be" Fred in my mind, and it didn't cost me much. Ben, on the other hand, represented the actual activity connected to dancing. He was trying to teach me—and a number of other hesitant husbands—to Lindy Hop. And when I stepped on the dance floor, Ben became pain personified.

From the moment Ben said, "Hi," I was sick to my stomach. Rescue became my top priority. I wondered how I could get out of the lessons without losing my wife. I thought about going back to the theology of my youth and praying for the rapture. But I was stuck with smiling Ben for six weeks of the Lindy Hop and with a wife who loved every minute of the experience.

As the weeks of dance lessons rolled on, I discovered something about myself. I'm not a dancer. I don't mean I'm not good at dancing, which is also a fact. I mean that inside me, at the core of who I am, *I am not a dancer.* It just isn't me. Oh sure, I can do it, just as I can "do" peas or sauerkraut. But it's not something I would choose to do, because it's not an activity remotely connected with who I am. Put me in front of thousands of people to speak, and I'm happy as a lark. Put me in a bookstore with a gift certificate, and I'm approaching nirvana. Put me in a coffeehouse with my computer, and I'm set for the next six hours or so. But put me on the dance floor, and I'll give new meaning to the word *squirm.*

Now before you think I'm just copping out of future dancing lessons, consider yourself. Think of an activity that is outside of your identity zone—not your comfort zone, but your identity zone. You avoid it, not because it's too difficult, but because it takes you too far from your center as a person. I bet that this banned activity is crystal clear in your mind. The reality is that we make choices in our lives about activities (what we do) based somewhat on our identities (who we are). And when it comes to *activities that fit,* I believe that churches are not that different from individuals.

Discovering *Your* Ministry

In Chapter 5, we discovered that *identity should precede activity.* It would also be true to say that *activity informs identity.* By trying certain activities (such as dancing), we discover more about who we are and who we are not. Your church's activity will spring most naturally from its communal identity. However, the various activities you try clue you in to that identity. The more these two align (who you are as a church and what you do as a church), the more potency your church will experience. The less these two align, the more scattered and ineffective your church will be.

Let's call the discovery and expression of activity your *ministry.* The current problem in many churches is that ministry activity is chosen with little or no regard for identity. That's why the issues in Chapter 5 should inform your conversation in this chapter. It's easy to simply dive into whatever activity is in style. This "try what's hot" method can leave your church out on a dance floor too far from its center. It also strangles effectiveness because the church's energy becomes too diffuse. On the other hand, some churches never experiment with ministry activity at all. This leads to a different kind of ineffectiveness: paralysis. It is only within the risk of experimentation that both identity and ministry can be confirmed.

The Trouble With Vision

In the last decade or so, churches have determined their ministry objectives by forming vision statements. These vision statements were often derived generically from a model "out there" or based on the success of a cool church. Unfortunately, this strategy doesn't take into account the unique identity of the church adopting the vision statement. To simply adopt a vision statement because it's generic enough to fit or because it has been successful somewhere else is missing the point of vision. It's a little like David trying to wear Saul's armor; it just didn't fit. David achieved mobility by discovering what fit him. Remember, vision is emergent, not static. You don't *adopt* it (as if it were armor); you *discover* it (as you move along).

The ministry of your church has to fit your church. And this brings us back to dancing. Churches, like individuals, have resonance meters. When you act *from* your communal identity, your resonance meter will go up. There will be a deep sense that you're accomplishing something of your essence. However, when you act *outside* of that identity, you will lose

Conversation Starters

• Do you agree that churches, like individuals, have resonance meters? Give an example of a ministry activity that resonates deeply with your church, versus one that was tried but created dissonance.

• Would you describe your ministry objectives (activity) as static or fluid? Give evidence to support your answer.

• How well do you believe your community responds to the fluctuations of ministry opportunities? What one quality would create more flexibility on your team or in your church with regard to the morphing of ministry?

• How closely aligned is your church's identity (who it is) with its ministry (what it does)?

your resonance and desire. Also, it's important to remember that ministry activity will morph with the different seasons of your church's life. The conversation around ministry requires *ongoing* exploration. Ministry objectives, once determined, do not remain static, but rather must remain fluid in order to respond to the times and the voice of the Spirit.

The Lenses of Ministry Discovery

The question before us at this point is "How do we discover the alignment between who we are and what we do as a church?" There are several lenses your church can look through to discover the ministry activity that best fits its emerging identity. Let me use an example from my own ministry experience at North Way to describe each lens. However, it is important at the outset to acknowledge that these lenses work best in concert. Making a decision based on one lens alone will not provide a rounded enough picture. When the lenses are simultaneously applied, the fidelity of the picture increases.

Remember, this is not so much about finding an overall ministry direction (although that could occur through the lenses) as it is about discovering the activities that are unique to your actionspace.

SETTING THE STAGE

A few years ago, I took on the role of overseeing the spiritual formation ministries at North Way. When my team and I began to assume responsibility for these ministries, we decided that we would not make any quick changes, knowing that, in fact, changes would come. To be honest, part of that decision was based on a healthy ignorance on my part. I knew changes were needed, but I wasn't sure what the changes should look like or what to change first. I needed some time to watch.

By the time this transition occurred, I'd been at the church over six years, so I wasn't unfamiliar with the history of these ministries. Up to that point, the bread and butter of those ministries had been seasonal adult-education classes and seminars that sought to speak to a variety of felt needs. These were six- to eight-week classes that were primarily, if not exclusively, held on the campus.

Early in the transition, my team and I had a hunch that something with this delivery mechanism needed to change. We decided initially, though, not to touch it. Instead, we poured our energy into making it successful. We stayed with the class format for about a year. During this first year, my team and I had a number of dynamic dialogues with people at North Way. Our desire was to listen and learn from the members. We did. As we listened, our hunch was vocalized again and again and became concrete and identifiable. We discovered something about our delivery mechanism (ministry activity) that was in direct opposition to our identity as a community.

LENS 1: MAXIMUM EFFECT

As my team and I moved more deeply into the ministry activity that was in place, we found teachers and facilitators pouring their hearts and souls into classes attended by only ten to forty people. Every so often a class would grow based on the popularity of the teacher, but the numbers never represented a very large percentage of the overall church. Soon I was hearing from my team, "We worked our fingers to the bone, and ten people showed up." Or, "After all this effort, attendance has fallen from fifty to twenty by the sixth week."

(Two comments are important here. First, some environments should be small in order to accomplish the aim of the experience. I'm not against smallness. Second, there can be a number of reasons for class attrition. I had to make sure attrition wasn't occurring because the experience was poorly executed. And it was not.)

Further, my team noticed that our ministry activity was going unnoticed by a large segment of our church. As we discussed all this with various members and as a team, we concluded that we were fighting against the deeper nature of our church. The deeper cultural value was small groups. For many years, the small group had been the locus of community and spiritual growth. It's not that growth couldn't occur outside a small group, but North Way chose to make small groups the critical engine of its communal connection and spiritual development.

At the time of this transition, at least fifteen hundred of the three thousand people who attend the church were in small groups (the percentage of small-group involvement has since increased). Because it takes time and energy to meaningfully participate in a small group, people were voting "no" to our educational opportunities. The reasoning went something like this: "I can be in a small group each week, but not in a small group *and* a weekly class, even for eight weeks." It's not that people didn't like the things we were doing in our classes and seminars; they just didn't have time for the small group and our classes.

Based on the need to affect as many people as possible, it became clear that our ministry activity was not potent. We were unable to expose a large segment of our community to the great content and facilitators in our actionspace. Class environments have their place, but our team realized we would never reach our community if the locus of our ministry activity didn't change.

The first lens is not necessarily about increasing the number of people you influence, but about increasing the overall effectiveness of your ministry activity. This will often include maximizing numbers (as in my case), but maximum effect could require you to decrease numbers. It all depends on what the ministry activity is meant to accomplish.

Your ministry activity itself gives you clues about effectiveness and the potential need for change. At some point, activity can become futile. But in times of ministry futility, don't overlook the possibility that the futility itself may be a gift inviting you to a better place.

The greatest sign of maximum effect is not numerical; it is change that renews the heart and energizes the hands. Maximum effect means maximum potency. It takes discernment to know when maximum effect will not translate into maximum numbers in a given situation. It takes courage to follow through in these situations because it is all too easy to be driven by the numbers.

> The greatest sign of maximum effect is not numerical; it is change that renews the heart and energizes the hands.

LENS 2: THE NEED RIGHT IN FRONT OF YOU

At the same time that my team was discovering that change was in the air, one of my colleagues, Bob, and his team were frustrated by a need they didn't have time to meet. Bob and his team, who oversee the small-group network at North Way, were having trouble finding creative, meaningful spiritual growth resources and experiences for small groups. As Bob and his team spent more and more time searching for good studies, my team and I spent more and more time searching for ways to entice members back to the building for another class or seminar.

Bob asked my team if we would help him find studies for the small groups. We said yes but secretly knew we wouldn't be able to give it too much time in light of all the classes and seminars we were developing. As my team searched for good studies, we discovered just how many mediocre studies are out there. Even the good studies didn't always speak to our church's unique situation. "If only the studies were tailored to the needs of our church. If only the studies were tailored to our small groups, like the classes and seminars we develop are tailored to those needs," we thought.

The people in small groups began asking for better-tailored resources as well. People would attend one of our classes,

Conversation Starters }

- Do you see instances in your ministry activity in which futility may be inviting you to change?

- If that futility had a voice, what would it be saying to you?

- Do you see any other signs indicating that change is warranted?

- Describe a time when maximum effect didn't translate into maximum numbers. Describe a time when maximum effect *did* translate into maximum numbers. What were the differences between these two situations? What can they teach you about the role of numbers in Lens 1?

seminars, or retreats and tell us that they wished their small groups could have shared the experience with them. Others asked if we might consider taking their small groups through the experience. We would respond by encouraging them to bring their small groups to the experience the next time it was offered. Even as we made this suggestion, we knew it was highly unlikely that small groups would make the time for the experience. Somehow we needed to reproduce the class or retreat so that it was portable and repeatable.

Determining your ministry's activity requires you to discern the needs in your actionspace, but you can't meet all of those needs. This is why viewing your ministry through one lens will not produce the best overall picture. The needs to pay attention to are the ones that lead you back to your identity and away from futility.

In my example, the futility of my situation intersected with the need of my colleague Bob. There was a direct connection between two needs: my need to maximize my team's influence and Bob's need to maximize resources to strengthen small-group growth. The whole situation reminded me of the old Reese's peanut butter cup commercials in

Conversation Starters

- When you examine your current ministry activity and actionspace, do you see any intersection of needs?

- Is there a need somewhere in your actionspace that could be met by a team in transition or one that is experiencing the futility of an activity that no longer fits your church? How could you move that team away from the futility and toward that pressing need?

which one person had the chocolate and the other had the peanut butter. Together they had...well, you know. What's important in Lens 2 is to discover that intersection of needs.

LENS 3: EMERGENCE

As this first year of transition unfolded, it seemed as though everything was moving toward a certain directional change. Perhaps as you read this, it's easy to see what we did. But remember, in the midst of discovering ministry, it's not always clear what is emerging. What's clear is that something is emerging, and the lenses can help you identify it.

For my team, fluid forces were moving in concert to reveal the bigger picture of what was to come. The messages from the overall community, Bob's need for resources, and my team's intuitive hunches were all pointing to a change of focus in our ministry. This is emergence. As I mentioned earlier, we are not the only artists. God is also at work in situations, relationships, and dynamics, arranging and rearranging. As the rearranging occurs, a new shape provides the team with the necessary energy to fulfill the emerging vision.

Many churches overlook emergence because they are too wedded to their current ministry models. It would have been much easier for my team to simply reinvent the old delivery mechanism of classes and seminars than to consider abandoning it. Everyone was comfortable with the old mechanism because it was familiar. I knew that if I pushed on it hard enough, I could have continued to prop it up. In the long run, though, it would not have succeeded because doing so would have meant losing ground and ignoring what *was* emerging: a new primary delivery system for our ministry.

Emergence invites us to let go of the trapeze of familiar activity in order to embrace a new form of activity that fits our identity. But many churches won't face the in-between time in which there is nothing to hold. Instead, they abandon the emerging vision and stay in Egypt, where all is predictable.

Watching for the emergence is part of the discovery process. Too many leaders and teams make the mistake of assuming they can make the decision about ministry issues without reading the moment. Not enough care is given to discerning the moment and what is springing from it.

Conversation Starters

• What are you noticing about your ministry? What's unfolding before your eyes? What do you see that is a clue to the next season of your activity?

Oftentimes, mistakes are made in leadership and in ministry because of an inability to read the moment with discernment and wisdom. One of the greatest skills of leaders and members engaged in the discovery of vision is the skill of seeing. Perhaps it is the most fundamental part of vision—the ability to see what is emerging and move with that emergence. Learning to pay attention is one of the greatest of all gifts, one that sharpens the vision of any team or community.

EXPERIENCEercise

Try to locate a Magic Eye 3-D picture. I'm talking about the pictures that first appear to be nothing more than a random collection of dots, but if you know how to look, they become so much more. You can visit the Web site www.magiceye.com for examples. Ask your team to scrutinize several of these pictures, and then talk about the similarities between seeing in 3-D and seeing the emerging vision of your community.

LENS 4: GIFT MIX

Around the same time I was given the responsibility to oversee the spiritual formation ministries, I hired an associate to work with our team and me. I had known Sue for a few years before hiring her. She had a great grasp of the kind of spiritual formation ministry that was important to me, and her own experience would be valuable to our culture. She had a deep sense of the contemplative aspect of spiritual formation (which I knew our church needed), and she was a writer. All of these things made her exactly the wrong candidate for the job as it stood in the old world of classes, retreats, and seminars.

But I knew intuitively that she was exactly the right person for the job.

A year into the transition, it all began to make sense. Although Sue had pulled off many excellent classes and seminars, she was constantly depleted by the hard work necessary to plan and execute those events. She was also discouraged by the lack of effect. Her primary gifts were languishing while she developed the old delivery mechanism.

I sat down with Sue and talked about her frustration and need for change. It was almost as if her own personal frustration was tied to the larger frustration of the ministry. I knew the change was close because of the amount of depletion and frustration infecting Sue and the wider team.

We began to see that providing small groups with quality curricula and materials aligned with Sue's gifts and passion. As the need in front of us grew, Sue's desire to meet that need through her gifting increased. The gifts needed to resource small groups were on my team, not Bob's. And yet the old way of doing things was an obstacle to the release of those gifts. Our team had the writers and teachers that could develop curriculum, but without an activity shift, those gifts would continue to languish.

The fourth lens allows us to evaluate the people on the team or in the church. I realized that part of what was depleting my team was the realization that each member was too far outside the center of his or her giftedness. And only as those gifts were activated and unleashed would the ministry change to accommodate those gifts. Leaders often believe that *need* should constitute *gift*. I believe it's just the opposite. Gifting leads you to the right need. Your unique activity will reflect the distinctive gifts of those in your actionspace. Let them lead you to the need and to the unique expression of your church's ministry.

LENS 5: FINDING THE RIGHT LANGUAGE

At some point, my team was confident that it was time to initiate the change. Conversations throughout our church had revealed that a cultural shift was needed to effect broad, meaningful spiritual formation. What we now needed was the language that would describe the new ministry to other leaders and the church at large. And so we expressed all that had been emerging in concrete language that would lead to action.

We no longer viewed the spiritual formation ministries as event-driven (seminars, workshops, and classes) but rather as resource- and experience-driven material for small groups. Instead of giving primary energy to ministry on campus, we would spend our time developing, writing, and producing print, video, and online curriculum that small groups could use to stimulate growth off campus.

We shared this idea with many of the people who had participated in the yearlong dialogue. When we did, it was as if the hidden image in a 3-D picture popped out at them. Not only did it make sense, but it also created an excitement that translated into passion. But without vocalizing the ideas, the image would have remained diffused.

Lens 5 is about the need to find the appropriate words to describe the unique activity you've discovered. Clear, specific language is needed to

Conversation Starters

- What areas of your ministry activity are losing steam because of a lack of clear language?

- We've already discovered that certain times of ambiguity are necessary for the discovery of vision. However, there comes a time when clarity is required if vision is to move forward. Are there areas of ambiguity in your ministry activities that are the result of unclear language? Name those areas.

make the intangible tangible, especially when a specific ministry activity is in transition. As your church and/or team discovers a part of its unique ministry, it is important to make explicit what has been tacit. Ambiguity is a necessary part of discovery, but at the right time, language is essential to make the idea concrete and achievable.

As you describe ministry activity, make certain that you don't turn the language into rigid labels that will block the very flexibility you want to cultivate. It's important to hold language loosely, or it can inhibit the next transformation. When we lock language in, it becomes a rigid label rather than a meaningful and flexible representation of reality. Think about language as the boundaries of a garden; you need the boundaries in order to stimulate growth, but the growth is far more than the boundaries. The boundaries simply enable the growth.

EXPERIENCEercise

Take some time as a team to describe the ministry activity that is unclear. Describe its purpose or reason for existing. Be as clear and succinct as you can. To help you do this, pretend you are sharing with a person who knows nothing about your ministry and you have the amount of time it would take to ascend ten floors in an elevator to describe it.

LENS 6: ENERGY, ENERGY, ENERGY

In my example, one of the immediate and positive consequences of the ministry change was energy. Everyone involved felt that the new piece of ministry fit who we were and made it more clear to them how their roles were connected to that ministry. My colleague Bob was ecstatic because he was no longer scrambling to find spiritual growth resources. For the first several months of the transition, every time I saw Bob he would smile and say, "You have no idea the difference your team is making." Bob showered my team with gratitude and me with lattes. I knew we were really making a difference in his ability to do his job with greater focus and vigor. It showed.

The members of my team were pumped up because they saw their work affecting a much larger segment of the church. In fact, thanks to the new ministry mechanism, we've created studies that two thousand people have simultaneously experienced. There would have been no way for this to occur in the other paradigm. My team also uses its gifts in ways the older ministry would not allow. We still offer a limited number of classes and other events, but now they are targeted at groups that need the content to be delivered in a more formal setting.

Experiencing renewed energy substantiates the fact that your ministry activity is potent and worthy of your time. Lens 6 helps point you to your unique ministry because it provides the fuel necessary to make it a reality. The right ministry expression for your actionspace will create energy inside individuals and momentum throughout the team and church. As much as futility can mark the end of ministry, energy can mark the beginning of a new season of ministry. It's as if the wind rises again, providing the vitality needed to fill the sail.

Conversation Starters

- What areas of your ministry activity are causing dissonance? What's the message behind this dissonance? Could it be time to let something end?

- Do you see a renewal of energy on your team or in your community that is the result of a certain ministry activity? How could you accent that energy and ministry in order to give it more space (and grace) to thrive?

Don't let a depletion of energy discourage you. Instead, allow it to lead you to a new discovery that will resonate with the members of your team and church. This may take some wandering in the desert, but it's worth it in the long run.

> The more resonance, the more energy.

Renewed energy is directly connected to the resonance I wrote about earlier. The more resonance, the more energy. Conversely, the more dissonance, the less energy. Energy depletion and renewal must be part of the conversation of ministry activity because they are so connected to our identity as individuals and as communities.

LENS 7: COMMUNAL PERSONALITY

One more lens is essential to this discussion. The ministry shift I described in my example absolutely fit our community. The small groups responded with delight. It met a real need these groups had

Conversation Starters

- Is your church engaged in specific ministry activities that don't fit its larger personality? Why do you think you engage in these ministries? Perhaps there is a good reason to keep them, but have you really evaluated them in light of the personality and calling of your church? Is it time to let them go?

- Can you locate a micro (team or group) pattern that fits your church's overall pattern? In other words, which of your church's ministry activities fits who it is? How can you maximize these activities and heighten their integration into your community?

been feeling for many years. The small-group world is the world of North Way. It certainly doesn't fully describe who North Way is or who it is becoming. But it does represent a deep cultural value that shapes the identity of the church. The shift in ministry activity allowed my team to align itself more with this collective identity. And that made all the difference in the world.

The final lens validates your ministry activity because it helps to determine if it resonates with your church. What the members of my team discovered was not only good for each of them, but it turned out to be exactly what the larger community needed. What worked at the micro level also worked at the macro level because it emerged from our communal identity.

This idea takes us back to the concept of fractals, or patterns. What was good for my team was also good for the whole. The new pattern of my team (the new way we do ministry) was more in line with the overall pattern of North Way. The micro pattern fit the personality of the macro pattern, and that created potency all over the place.

EXPERIENCEercise

Make a "stop-doing" list of those ministries that don't resonate with your communal identity. Then make a to-do list of those that *do* resonate and should be maximized. What character traits are required to accomplish both lists? What dangers do you face in eliminating the ministry activities on the stop-doing list?

Be careful not to end activities without wisdom and discretion. But neither should you be bound by ministry activities that drain your teams and your members.

One Small Caution

The illustration I chose to use in this chapter focused on the need for change in our ministries. But the seven lenses are just as useful in helping a church determine if it should keep certain ministry activities instead of changing them. The goal is not always to change, but rather to use the lenses to evaluate the emerging activity of your ministry. The lenses enable you to move when it's time to move and stay put when it's time to dig more deeply. Don't use the lenses to come up with conclusions similar to mine. Use them to discern what's unfolding in your own actionspace.

CHAPTER 7

CONVERSING ABOUT MOTION: Is Your Church Maximizing Its Communal Energy?

Pushing Too Hard

"I'M IN A GROOVE," I thought to myself as I backed the truck out of the driveway. As it was December, I was leaving the house long before the sun would awaken the day. I had set aside a few early morning hours to write the first draft of the chapter you are about to read. My early morning writing normally occurs at Starbucks because it is the portal between heaven and earth. So off I went.

I had a few voice mail messages to leave for colleagues that morning, so I decided to deliver them from my hands-free phone while driving to Starbucks. As I left the final message, I felt a tremendous sense of peace, anticipation, and adrenaline flowing through me. In the last several days, I had written far more than I had thought possible, and I was energized by the prospect of accomplishing another large chunk of writing.

Just then, the truck I was driving suddenly lost all power. As I was waiting at a stoplight, every system failed simultaneously. There was nothing but the glow of the red stoplight coming off my hood and a number of approaching headlights in my rearview mirror. I tried to start the truck a couple of times, but to no avail. I then realized I had a small window of time to enact plan B before the traffic behind me became the traffic upon me.

Spying a gas station off to my right, I began pushing the Ford Ranger down a slope toward it. I picked up enough steam to get the truck off the street and just barely into the parking lot. When I ran out of strength, though, I was still a ways from an actual parking spot. A good Samaritan saw my plight, and together we struggled to push the tank to a safe spot.

It had been some time since I had been in a situation like this. Although car breakdowns were a weekly occurrence in college, those days are long gone. When I had finished pushing, I was depleted. After my car was safely parked, I noticed that I was within walking distance of a different Starbucks. There is a God. I was close enough to walk to the Starbucks and perhaps still get some writing in before calling home to inform my wife that her morning plans were going to change.

I don't believe in coincidences. I am much more comfortable with a view of the world that includes divine synchronicity rather than random chance. So as I sat down to begin writing, I paused to ask myself, "Why did this happen *this* morning?" As I thought about the ordeal, it all seemed too easy. The light was red; the cars were far enough behind me to allow me time to push. The good Samaritan showed up just at the right moment. And the Starbucks was within walking distance. All this caused me to wonder if the experience was supposed to shape my morning writing rather than end it. "What's the message, God?" I wondered.

As I sat there listening, I felt as though God nudged me. "Do you feel the strain in your body from pushing?"

That was an easy answer: "Yes!"

The nudge continued, "That's how many in the church feel these days." It dawned on me that many people in churches all across the United States (and beyond) have been anxiously pushing their ministries for many years. I realized that the overall condition of church people might be similar to the condition of my body after the morning strain: depleted.

Pushing most ministries requires a tremendous amount of energy, and this has taken a toll on leaders and members alike. Without some kind of transformation in this area, the future may be lined with burned out, bitter Christ-followers who give up on ministry in order to protect the little energy they have left.

The toll that this kind of depletion produces extends beyond the moment of strain. As I made my way through the car-troubled morning, I noticed different parts of my body protesting. All of the pain didn't show up at once. After the initial strain, the pain became more pronounced in certain areas of my body. When people strain too hard to sustain ministry, the pain is felt for some time. Yet many have no time to slow down and let the aches subside. It's always time to push again. When there's no rest, people get perpetual kinks in their necks, and when they minister, they are just a bit out of whack.

What I'm Not Saying: The Trap of Extremes

I've discovered that when people discuss this issue of motion—energy given to further the ministry—they tend toward one of two extremes. On the one hand, it's easy to fall prey to the thinking that the ministry of a church, from a programmatic standpoint, should be almost nonexistent. These are the minimalists. They believe that you should simply nourish and nurture people and let them be ministers at work and in their neighborhoods. "Don't overload people with so much activity at church that they have no time to love the people around them, not to mention their families," the minimalists would say. Of course there is some—no, a lot—of truth in this view.

On the other side of the debate are the "kingdom commandos." They push even harder when told that people might be burned out. Commandos believe that God is concerned with only the church and that there is nothing more important than advancing its agenda. Believing as they do, they wonder how anyone could question the wholehearted investment necessary to advance the kingdom. To a commando, concerns about time or energy expose a frailty that can be remedied only by getting more involved. There are some fragments of truth in this view as well. The problem is that the extreme nature of both positions prevents people from entering a dynamic dialogue about energy.

The modern church has constructed a ministry structure that is more a reflection of the modern mind-set than anything else. We've justified our propensity toward *over*activity on the grounds that people need spiritual growth or their eternal destinies hang in the balance or...or...or... Yet Jesus exhibited none of this way of thinking or behaving. He never used car salesmen–like techniques to get people to buy into a mandate or mission. Many of the tactics in the modern church are the result of leaders who created more work than they could personally sustain. And so the work has fallen to the members. Often this work is neither an offshoot of the communal identity nor activity that will lead to authentic spiritual growth; it stems from the dreams and aspirations of church leaders.

On the other hand, we live in a relatively selfish culture. We tend to view our time as *our time*. For the most part, we don't feel we should have to give an account to anyone for the way we choose to spend it.

Robert Bellah and others, in their book *Habits of the Heart,* have revealed to us with deftness and thoughtfulness the dangers of individualism and a mind-set that views community as nothing but an afterthought for busy and rugged individualists.

The lack of true community—which would include communal motion and energy—in the church only suggests to those around us that we, too, are primarily interested in our own ventures rather than in communal ones. A significant amount of the New Testament is written to the collective church rather than to the individuals who make up the collective. Paul goes out of his way to stress the communal nature of the church. Some would go as far as to suggest that salvation is a communal matter before it is an individual matter.

Why Does This Happen?

The frenetic pace in many churches is due first to the fact that people don't know how to converse. And second, it is the result of a misunderstanding of their mission identity and ministry activity. Churches composed of people who don't know who they are collectively end up chasing a number of ideas and directions that initially sound good but end up depleting the church rather than energizing it. These groups only know how to say yes because they don't understand that their energy must be localized and narrowed if it is to be potent.

Another reason the motion level of many churches is off the scale is because the leaders of those churches haven't learned how to distinguish the difference between their personal dreams and communal ministry. Too many times, as I mentioned earlier, a church's identity is enmeshed with that of its senior leader or leaders. Though some identity convergence is quite healthy, the church must be more than the sum of its leaders.

Many pastors and leaders have personal ambitions that too easily become communal endeavors. I'm not suggesting a pastor's personal vision cannot merge quite nicely with a church's calling, but this should be discovered through dialogue rather than the unstoppable will of the leader. Some leaders preach community and sacrifice for the whole but are really calling people to sacrifice for something that is nothing more than their own personal dreams. This is hypocrisy.

Of course, people who do not hold formal positions of leadership can just as easily push agendas that don't resonate with community identity. These people can make it difficult for anyone who challenges the validity of their ministry ideas. They expect their churches to throw their resources and energy behind their ideas. This occurs more readily in small churches, but large churches aren't immune. The longer and more intensely people serve, the greater their opportunities are to move their own agendas forward. Grace and unselfishness must mark the members of a church as much as its leaders.

The Flow of Motion—Giving and Receiving: You've Gotta Have Both

Healthy organisms give and receive. In fact, it is through the rhythm of giving and receiving that energy is renewed. Both motions are necessary in order to sustain vitality and create wholeness. If a person expends too much energy, the result is depletion. On the other hand, if too little energy is expended, the result is also depletion. We normally call this second kind of depletion *lethargy*. As human beings, we all must learn to find that rhythm point between burnout due to too much activity and burnout due to inactivity.

> As churches, we must learn to inhale (receive) and exhale (give).

Think about breathing. Imagine what it would be like if you could only inhale. Life would get impossible in a hurry. Of course, the reverse—constant exhaling—would be no better. There is a rhythm to breathing, and we need both components of the rhythm to maintain health. As people, we take breathing for granted; we do it automatically. But as churches, we must learn to inhale (receive) and exhale (give). And we must learn to discern the point in between (the pause).

Communities that spend all their time giving will soon have nothing left to give. Or their ministry activities will become a drag in every way possible. Of course, communities that are in perpetual "take mode" and see no reason to reach beyond their own walls become a collective version of Jabba the Hutt—large lumps of self-indulgent flesh.

Before we go on, try this: Take a deep breath, and then exhale. Did you notice the three motions of your breathing? First, you inhaled, and then there was a momentary but important pause. And finally, you exhaled. I want to use these three movements as a metaphor to help you discover the unique energy level and energy expression of your church. It is critical to dialogue around all three parts: the inhale (receive/rest), the exhale (give/share), and the pause in the middle (the season in between). We'll begin our look at these three movements with the inhale, because without drawing something in, there is nothing to give out. However, ultimately these motions must work synergistically in an unbroken cycle. Each one complements and enables the other.

INHALE: REST, REFLECT, AND CELEBRATE

The inhale is the first movement of energy supply. Rest, reflection, and celebration are the activities that re-energize the church. As the church inhales, it discovers an appreciation for what *is* and becomes replenished for what is to come. It's easy to come off a time of high ministry activity and forget to inhale. Driven to distraction, we instead may simply ask, "What's next?" This is a mistake of the worst kind. It only perpetuates the kind of frenetic pace I described earlier.

Appreciation for What *Is*

Gratitude and appreciation for what God has done in your church is the foundation for renewable energy. It's important that your appreciation become an intentional part of your inhale. Because of our penchant for quickly moving on to the next exhale, it's easy to miss the collective moment of appreciation for what has happened and is happening in your actionspace.

During a communal inhale, the community creates space for replenishment and rejuvenation. Because space and pace are directly connected to each other, when communal space is made, the pace of the church tends to slow. This slower pace enables the church to take part in the activities of the inhale. Rest and reflection create the space and grace your church needs.

Conversation Starters

- Discuss how your church handles various holidays and holy days. Do you pack them with events so that there is no space for members and leaders to consider the wonder of the season at hand?

- If this is your church's pattern, how do you think it has come about?

- Are you satisfied with the results this pattern is giving you?

- Do you give your ministry leaders and servants sufficient rest?

- Scrutinize your ministry calendar. Have times been set aside for rest? If they haven't been, why not?

Rest

After a time of intense ministry activity—on a team or within an entire church—rest is critical to ongoing health. It is unhealthy to move at full speed for prolonged times without rest. The rest I'm referring to here is far more than a momentary break. It is a restoration that literally puts us back together. Activity, whether individual or collective, has a way of *dis*integrating us. This *dis*integration is unavoidable. It is, at one level, the nature of activity that it pulls us apart or fractures our energy. Rest then reintegrates us and provides us with the vitality we need to exhale.

> Without intentional respites, a church becomes addicted to motion, and that can lead it to put its trust in its own energy rather than God's.

Without intentional respites, a church becomes addicted to motion, and that can lead it to put its trust in its own energy rather than God's. The danger in community life is the belief that group energy is never depleted. But this is not true. Communities, like individuals, grow weary and need rest. I believe restless communities may in fact have a harder time trusting God, because they are used to doing it all themselves. When a community rests, it sends a powerful message about the vulnerability of the people and the sufficiency of their Creator.

As you read this section, you may wonder what I mean by *rest*. "Do we all take a collective nap, or what?" Here are some ways to foster moments of collective rest.

There are times of intense activity in the church—holidays or holy days, for example. We pack these times so full of events that their deeper meaning may be lost. Christmas is a pet peeve of mine. Who made the decision that Christmas would be a time to run members ragged with so many rehearsals and events that the meaning of the season is lost? Is it possible to have a meaningful community celebration without demanding so much of members?

The season of Advent is almost nonexistent in a number of Protestant circles. The deeper messages of waiting and anticipation, hope and wonder are lost in busyness. But churches can foster rest by reserving some time during this and other holidays for people to personally contemplate the meaning of the season at hand.

I encourage you to make space in the calendar and intentionally invite your congregation to use the space to consider the season upon them. I'm already hinting here at the second activity of the inhale: reflection. But before reflection is possible, space must be made for it and the heart must be prepared for it.

Another way to rest is to occasionally cancel all your weekly ministries. Like a field, your actionspace occasionally requires rest in order to remain fertile in the long run. Canceling the ongoing ministries of your church for a specific period of time gives those involved in those ministries the chance to rest and be renewed for the days ahead.

{ EXPERIENCE ercise }

There are many ways to rest within your actionspace besides canceling or reducing the number of events. Your team knows your church and its needs. As a team, brainstorm five ways you could rest your church in the coming six months. Then choose the best way to breathe space and grace into your ministry activity.

Reflection

Another important part of receiving is reflection. Reflection is an activity that we do only if we've made space for it. It helps us to find the meaning in our experiences. This is a time to gain perspective on the collective journey, to relish the faithfulness of God, and to pull a few threads together that may have unraveled during the time of exhaling.

Reflection also enables us to appreciate what *was* and *is* before moving to what *could be*. As we reflect, we honor the past, learn from it, and allow the Spirit time to shape our character—which in turn readies us for the future. Reflection keeps us from treating past ministry activity like an old exercise machine that gathers dust in the basement. As we uncover the meaning of past ministry activity, it gives us greater insight into the days ahead.

{ EXPERIENCE ercise }

Along with personal reflection times, there are some very specific ways your church can reflect in concert throughout its journey. Here's one example.

Healthy churches tell stories about their histories and about their journeys as they unfold. Here are a couple of ways to prompt storytelling in your midst.

Stories about your church's roots—As a team (or congregation), tell the story of your church's history. Trace the story as far back as you can. Let those with the most history tell their stories of the past and how, from their perspectives, God has worked in the church through the years. Paint as complete a picture of your church's history as possible.

Stories about God's faithfulness—Encourage the congregation or your team to tell stories that remind you of God's faithfulness. All churches have stories about God's deliverance and his creative work in their midst. These stories should be occasionally retold to renew trust in God and his purposes. Telling these stories also reminds the church that there is more to communal life than "the next thing." It prevents the church from engaging in activity for activity's sake. When we value the past, we treat the present and the future with more care. Remembering the past also lessens anxiety because it reminds us that God is present and still working as he always has.

It's important to occasionally tell these stories when the entire congregation is gathered. This keeps the collective attention aimed at the right things. You can do both of these Experiencercises in a team setting or during a time of communitywide celebration.

Celebration

If reflection leads to a collective understanding of the significance of a certain season, then celebration is a collective *wonder*standing in the presence of God, the true champion of any ministry activity. Times of communal worship to give thanks and celebrate seasons of ministry are essential.

Celebration and worship bring the church into focus and put God and his faithfulness at the center of our attention. Just as the children of Israel celebrated God after a time of battle or trial, so your church should celebrate God after a fruitful time of ministry.

EXHALE

In Chapter 6, we discussed many of the elements of exhaling, that is, ministry activity. In Chapter 5, we discussed where this takes place—your mission's actionspace. Now let's turn our attention to two qualities that should be a part of every exhale, regardless of the specific activity or its actionspace.

Conversation Starters

• Which of these two virtues—life and love—may be lacking in your ministry activity?

Every time the church exhales, its aim should be to share life—the abundant life of Jesus. Exhaling ministry activity without life is just bad breath. Unfortunately, there is a lot of halitosis coming from the church today. Though activity abounds, much of it lacks life. Jesus' ministry was attractive because of the life connected to it. In everything he did, Jesus brought life to the moment. The activity changed according to the situation, but the life remained consistent in every circumstance. Life is the creative expression of the Spirit made manifest in the moment of need.

Without rest, reflection, and celebration, there's just not much life in the next exhale. An empty well is of no use to a thirsty person.

Along with life, each exhale should be filled with love. Without love, Paul likened ministry activity to a one-dimensional noise—a gong. If life is the creative expression of the Spirit, then love is the compassion that makes the expression others-centered. Love keeps our energy focused outward and driven by compassion, mercy, and grace.

EXPERIENCEercise

In the days ahead, keep your eyes open for different ministry activities that occur on your team or in your church. Notice if life and love infuse that action, or if it seems more as if people are simply going through the motions. After you observe these situations, write your observations down or share them with your team.

- What evidence of life and/or love did you notice?

- How could you increase these two virtues throughout the ministry activity of your actionspace?

- If love or life was missing, what could you do to infuse the team and the activity with these virtues? Perhaps it's time to inhale.

THE PAUSE IN BETWEEN

As I mentioned earlier, there is a slight pause between the inhale and the exhale. In-between moments are important and certainly not throw-away moments in the production and renewal of energy. The in-between moment is a turning point from giving to receiving or from receiving to giving. Turning points invite us to the other side of the movement. It is then up to us to determine how we will respond. If the pause is coming at the end of the exhale, then it's time to rest, reflect, and celebrate. If the pause is coming at the end of the inhale, then it's time to engage in a new season of activity.

Pausing to Inhale

The sign that your church is pausing to inhale is the loss of collective energy to sustain the exhale. The ministry activity is coming to an end, and there is a sense that the church is on the other side of the wave.

Pausing to Exhale

The biggest sign that it's time to exhale is anticipation. Your church will sense that something new is about to happen. At this point, leaders must point the collective vision of the team or the church toward that new something and harness the energy that will unleash the exhale. Even more, when a community senses it is moving into a

Conversation Starters

- Can you identify certain ministry teams that need to inhale (rest, reflect, and celebrate)?

- What could you do to encourage this team to rest?

- Is your entire church in need of rest? Perhaps it's time for some conversations that lead to a time of space and grace.

season of intense ministry activity, it's important to keep the conversation alive by allowing members to participate in the preparation and execution of that new season.

{ Conversation Starters

- Can you identify a segment of your church's ministry activity that is poised to exhale?

- What can you do to encourage this?

- Is your entire church poised for an exhale? Perhaps it's time for some conversations that lead to action.

CHAPTER 8

CONVERSING ABOUT MONEY: Is Your Church OK With How Its Money Is Spent?

Holy Eavesdropping

I'VE HAD A FANTASY FOR MANY YEARS. Just about every time I'm in a church service and the offering is about to be taken, the fantasy kicks in. It's not terribly dramatic, but, boy, do I wish my fantasy were within the realm of possibility! My fantasy is to hear every person's thoughts as the money is collected. Would that be a kick, or what?

This fantasy springs, I suppose, from my experience with money and the church throughout my lifetime. As a pastor for nearly twenty years, I've heard many of the private thoughts of church members in my office or over lunch or coffee. If one is willing to listen, really listen, to people's ideas and concerns about money, the conversation will flow. If one is not in the mood to listen, but rather in the mood to convince the speaker of a particular viewpoint, the conversation dries up like a river crying for summer rain.

{ **EXPERIENCE**ercise }

As a group, discuss what you believe people in your church are thinking during the offering. Frame your answers so that they reflect what you think people would say about how the money they are about to give will be stewarded. For example, would someone think, "I sure hope this doesn't go toward our collection of six hundred microphones"? Or would someone think, "I hope our pastors are being adequately compensated"? Or, "No, God, not another building"?

Before doing this exercise, remember two things. First, the goal is for the group to simply wonder what people are thinking. It's not to judge those thoughts. Someone might have a problem with the number of microphones or buildings the church has, and that struggle could be his or her problem rather than a real one.

Second, you might be thinking this is a useless exercise because people should be thinking about nothing but God when they give. To that I would say, remember that your church is a community. Of course our giving should be filled with worship, but it should also be accompanied by thoughts of how the church's money can best be used. To suggest that people should have no thoughts at all about how the money is spent is a giant leadership cop-out.

In my conversations I've discovered that there are some prevailing patterns in the thoughts leaders and members have about money in the church. Leaders often harbor feelings of frustration over a lack of shared fiscal responsibility. Many leaders have said, "If everyone would pull his or her own weight, we would have more money than we would know what to do with." Leaders believe in the activity of their churches and realize that activity requires a fuel beyond human bodies; it requires money. Leaders also know that members who share the load lighten that load in significant ways. When this load sharing does not occur (which is often), leaders become frustrated, and this frustration is manifested in subtle ways in their speech and behavior.

On the other hand, many members are often suspicious about where the money is going and how it is being used. I do *not* mean to suggest that most people believe their leaders are misusing funds for personal gain. Rather, members often wonder if the church's money is being spent wisely. They may wonder because they don't really know where the money is going...or because they do. In other words, members wonder if the money is truly meeting the needs that the congregation supports.

Leaders tend to believe that once the money enters the plate, basket, or coffer, it is no longer within the purview of the people. They believe the people trust them with the money and that they are to be good stewards of it. They believe it would be impractical and even unwise to involve a large group of people in the church's money matters. This perspective does seem reasonable and has some truth to it.

Members, on the other hand, often don't have a forum by which to express questions and concerns about money. They may sense inequities in "whose voice is heard" in money matters. For example, those with the loudest voices might also happen to have the nicest cars.

All of these issues can easily eclipse the reason we give in the first place. We give because we love God and want to help people. The businesslike environment of the modern church has made it difficult to keep this the central heartbeat of our giving. This is not to suggest that we should abandon everything the modern church has become (although there's plenty we could jettison), but when Paul took up a collection for the poor in Jerusalem, the whole

> The poor are often not even on the radar screen in many church economies.

endeavor was simple. He visited churches, collected the money, and gave it to the poor. And the money he collected went to sustain the basic needs of life.

Giving today supports the basic needs of an organization. The poor are often not even on the radar screen in many church economies. Instead, mortgages, staff, debt, office furniture, computers, and programs are the primary targets. It is therefore trickier for both the giver and the steward as they consider their roles in this arrangement.

I know that many churches do wonderful things for the poor and hurting all over the world. My words are not meant in any way to cast a shadow on that good. Nor am I suggesting that the items I listed as primary expenditures are evil. However, the church as it exists today makes it hard on itself when it comes to giving. For the most part, leaders ask members to support something that appears more like a business than a distribution house for the needy and downtrodden. Consider this example:

Which of the following churches will have more struggles with giving and perception? Church A builds a simple structure to house its on-site ministries. It purposely keeps internal expenses low in order to give a significant amount of money to local and global efforts that feed the poor and help the hurting. Church B has every imaginable bell and whistle at its disposal. This allows Church B to speak the experiential language of postmoderns but also reduces its ability to venture into humanitarian efforts. Now stay with me...I didn't ask which church is better. And I'm not trying to subtly suggest that Church A is better. But the question is almost rhetorical. Church B will have a harder time—hands down. It's just harder to justify Disneyland when Jesus is pretty clear about the poor and broken.

{ EXPERIENCEercise }

SUPPLIES: a white board or a large sheet of paper and a marker

INSTRUCTIONS: On a large sheet of paper or a white board, draw a line down the center. On one side write "early church," and on the other write "our church." As a group, discuss the differences between the way money was used in the early church and the way it's used today. Write the differences on the paper or white board. After listing some of the differences, discuss which of them are merely cultural and which may supersede culture. What can the early church teach us about the use of money, and what could we teach the early church? The goal of the exercise is to determine if the usage of money in the church is purely cultural, or if we can discern wise principles that transcend culture and should shape the church's use of money regardless of the time period.

"Dave, Is This Going Somewhere?"

These ideas are in no way new. Members and leaders have wrestled with them for a long, long time. And the way I set up the concept naturally leads to polarization. One is almost forced to take a side and stick with it. Further, many American church leaders and members don't want to have this conversation (at least the way I set it up) because there doesn't seem to be any solution to the problem. Some might ask, "So are you saying we should sell our church, take the money, and send it to Africa?" This is the kind of discussion that often comes from polarization. What to do?

SHOULD WE HAVE THIS CONVERSATION?

The first issue a church must decide is if the conversation about money is an important part of the communal QUEST. If the conversation is viewed as important, the leaders and members of a church *can* find an effective, productive way to dialogue about it. But both groups will have to want to—without the "want to," the conversation won't last long and the attempt will be seen as a dismal failure. The first question is "Do we as a community want to have this conversation?" If the answer is no, nothing I can suggest will be of any value. The decision has already been made.

SUSPENSION

The second issue necessary for groups to consider if they want to converse about money is really more of a skill. Groups must learn the skill and art of suspending assumptions in order to move this conversation along. I have not yet talked about this skill. I decided to save it for this section because, although all conversations benefit from suspension, conversations about money seem to require this skill more than any other.

David Bohm describes suspension as the ability to suspend impulses and judgments during a dialogue. But suspending judgment, according to Bohm, does not mean suspending your feelings on a topic; rather, you share your feelings—as well as listen to others—without connecting those words to judgments:

> It does not mean repressing or suppressing or, even, postponing them. It means, simply, giving them your serious attention so that their structures can be noticed while they are actually taking place.

A certain kind of detachment is necessary for suspension to occur in a group conversation. Participants must be able to restrain their negative emotional reactions meant to control the content and direction of the discussion. We've all seen people's emotional reactions either shut down conversations or move them down a particular path. We've probably done this ourselves at one time or another. It's a conversational ploy we use when things aren't going the way we want them to go. And it's very easy to employ this tactic when talking about money in the church. That's why the rest of this chapter is devoted to ways that will help your team

> We've all seen people's emotional reactions either shut down conversations or move them down a particular path.

Conversation Starters

- Is the subject of money difficult to discuss in your church? Why or why not?

- Have you experienced a conversation about money in the church that didn't go so well? What led to the degeneration of the conversation?

- If you could have the conversation all over again, what, if anything, would you do differently?

- Do you agree with my characterization of leaders and members when it comes to money in the church? Did I exaggerate, or is the situation close to the way I described it?

- We're about to move into three sections that will teach us more about the art of suspension. Before we dive into these sections, how well do you think you practice suspension in difficult conversations?

or congregation understand the specifics of good suspension and relate them to conversations about money.

Before we consider the art of suspension in light of conversations about money, let me remind you that it is possible to engage your members (if you are a leader) in this conversation without suggesting that they get to make decisions about money in the church. Remember, this is not about dynamic *decisions*; it's about dynamic *discussions*. The Conversation Starters in the following sections can be implemented using any of the three structures I described in Chapter 4. Or you as a leader can simply call a number of members together to discuss this chapter. Let them know that you want their input and that input will not necessarily translate into execution. You're seeking their wisdom, not their decisions.

Cultivating Suspension

At the heart of suspension lie three important emotional qualities: honesty, equanimity, and pliability. Most of what blocks suspension is emotional in nature. Unhealthy emotional reactions surface when people are threatened by potential polarization. When this occurs, we dig in and ready ourselves to defend our positions. Lines are drawn, and the battle ensues. Real dialogue is not possible unless we can defuse this moment and learn to suspend these emotional reactions. To combat these reactions, people on a team must learn to cultivate the three emotional virtues. Let's look at the three virtues in light of the topic of money.

Honesty

When conversations get intense, we tend to hide. Some people hide by withdrawing from the conversation. Others end it by engaging more deeply in emotional ploys such as anger or domination. Some use humor or tears or other tactics to dilute the intensity. Whatever the tactic, the result is the same: The conversation is over.

The really annoying thing about all of this is that when we are conversing with others, we don't all use the same tactic to thwart the dialogue. This means that we are not only frustrated by the difficulty of the topic, but we also are aggravated by the ways others are thwarting the conversation. Their particular tactics of avoidance—different from our own—heighten our frustration.

I recently sat next to a mother and her daughter on a short flight from Phoenix to Tucson. As soon as they sat down, I knew things had not been going well for them. It was a late-night flight, every seat was taken, everyone was tired, and these two had been fighting. Their faces told the story and their desire for the night to end.

Before the plane had even lifted off, the tactics of emotional manipulation were in full swing. The daughter, who appeared to be about fourteen, went into zombie mode. She stared out the window with a look of depression that deflated the people seated in three rows around her. The zombie posture was no good for Mom. She wanted to talk and talk *now*. Mom, sensing she was not getting through, leaned into her daughter with more intensity. Out of the corner of my eye, I could see her head and body punctuating her muted tones. The more she came at her daughter in anger, the more her daughter stared out the window. They were irritating each other to no end, which in turn made them both dig in even more. And so the cycle continued as I watched them leave the airport in Tucson.

The real problem between the mom and the daughter is the same problem that many groups face when they discuss money. The mom and daughter could not suspend their emotional reactions long enough to hear each other's point of view. Leaders and members who want to dialogue about

> Leaders and members who want to dialogue about money must not allow the emotional nature of the conversation to thwart their ability to remain honest.

money must not allow the emotional nature of the conversation to thwart their ability to remain honest. Honesty, without emotional manipulation, allows a group to move further into the conversation.

Honesty requires that people remain committed to the QUEST, even when it seems that the QUEST is confusing (remember chaos; remember *kairos*). Emotional honesty requires a "stay with it" and a "stay open" attitude. One of the ways to remain honest in these moments is to simply be honest about the emotional reactions that are sabotaging the discussion. A simple statement can go a long way to defuse the

Conversation Starters

- Can you identify emotional reactions that thwart your team or congregation from authentic conversations?

- Often these emotional reactions surface at predictable moments in a conversation. Can you identify when they surface in your conversations? Describe these moments.

More Conversation About Money and Honesty

- Is it safe for members of your church to honestly express their feelings about the way money is stewarded? Or is there a subtle pressure to comply with the wishes of the leaders? If so, describe this honestly but without an emotional reaction.

- Is it safe for leaders in your church to challenge members about giving, or does it appear that the leaders are simply harping about money?

- Talk honestly about some of the reasons you are concerned about money in your church. Remember, the goal is not to get your way, but to find collective wisdom. Here are some possible topics:

  - Is the debt load in your church too high?

  - Is there a lack of a clear vision about stewardship?

  - Do you believe in the tithe, or is that now in opposition to New Testament grace?

  - Does your church have sufficient accountability in place to ensure wise money management?

moment. "Ya know, this is a pretty tough part of our conversation, and I sense we're all feeling a bit stressed right now. I just want you all to know, I'm committed to you and this process."

A statement like this is powerful because it brings the struggle out into the open where it can be defused. If it stays below the surface, the tense conversation can quickly become "the item we never discuss." Honesty about the tense moment goes a long way toward keeping honesty about the topic moving forward.

Another way to keep the honesty flowing is to foster a safe environment. If someone shares something difficult and is greeted by emotional manipulation, chances are good he or she won't share again. People get skittish after a few emotional bombardments. It becomes unsafe to share anything that could cause disagreement. Soon others receive the same message and clam up. What's left is a group that carefully avoids trouble spots in favor of the shallow waters of small talk and "must talks."

As a team or group, if you have a problem with this kind of honesty, it is best to discuss this weakness first, when you are not experiencing the problem. Take some time when things aren't emotionally charged to face this issue. Honesty about your lack of honesty is the first step in cultivating the virtue itself. Then you'll be in a much better position to discuss an issue such as money.

Equanimity

Equanimity is the second virtue that enables a group to cultivate suspension and dialogue about tricky topics. If you look up *equanimity* in a thesaurus, you'll find words like *calmness* and *composure* as synonyms. But that doesn't do true justice to the idea. Here's my shot at describing the word: Equanimity is the ability to be undisturbed by surface distraction. When the conversation is difficult, there are always lures near the surface that seek to undo the group's unity. These can be lures of content (a specific issue that is emotionally charged), or they can be lures of reaction (a specific person's emotional reaction to the topic).

> Equanimity is the ability to be undisturbed by surface distraction.

In these moments, we must learn to remain undisturbed, unaffected, disinterested, and even dispassionate about those lures. If the team reacts to the reactions of others, the cycle enlarges and the conversation unravels quickly. To converse with equanimity is to learn to be—at one level—dispassionate about very passionate topics. This doesn't mean that the team is indifferent to the topic or to one another; it means that the team doesn't engage in or respond to emotionally charged content or the emotional reactions of others.

A still or centered heart in the midst of the lure prevents each team member from succumbing to it and reminds the group of its commitment to the QUEST. There is so much at stake for the group if the QUEST is sabotaged by these lures. Therefore, the team's intention to cultivate equanimity must remain high. One way to do this is to remember the QUEST and the adventure the moment the lure appears. The lure is not worth the damage it could cause. Therefore

> To converse with equanimity is to learn to be—at one level—dispassionate about very passionate topics.

{ Conversation Starters

- Can you see ways in which your team or congregation is lured into responding emotionally?

- Name some of these lures. Does a certain topic always elicit a negative emotional response? Or do certain people act as lures for others on the team?

Answering these questions in a group setting can be tricky. If you don't feel your group can handle this conversation by itself, bring in an objective party who is skilled at helping groups through tough spots.

- What is one concrete action your team could take to increase its equanimity in difficult conversations?

More Conversation About Money and Equanimity

- Is money a topic that is laced with lures for your church or team? If so, why?

- Have you noticed people clashing over the topic?

- What is at the core of these lures? Are people afraid, wounded, or _____ (you fill in the blank) about money?

the team chooses to remain unaffected by it or at least works toward that end.

The virtue of equanimity is also tied into the necessity for group stillness and waiting. Both those virtues help to cultivate equanimity because they help us to be silent and wait in difficult conversational moments, rather than barging in with guns loaded.

{ EXPERIENCEercise }

Gather an appropriate group of members or a team from your church to discuss a monetary issue that is a sticky point for your church. Talk briefly about the virtue of equanimity before beginning the conversation. Ask participants to make a concerted effort not to respond to the emotional lures in the content or other individuals. Try to mine the collective wisdom of the group, bearing in mind that the goal is not to make a decision about the issue.

After the conversation, debrief it with the group. Ask specifically if equanimity made a difference in the conversation, and, if so, how. Ask people to give specific examples. The information you glean from this conversation will help you in future conversations about money. You may even want to make your insights available to others on your staff.

Pliability

The third virtue that helps to cultivate suspension is pliability. Emotional pliability is the ability to bend with others in a conversation, even if the ideas and convictions of others are different from your own. This doesn't mean that you necessarily agree with the other conversationalists. However, it does mean that you are able to go with them into their ideas and convictions without feeling threatened or disengaging from the topic.

Pliability is important to dynamic dialogue first, of course, because it helps to suspend emotional reaction. But pliability is also critical because

> Groups that cannot lean in the direction of different points of view fall quickly into groupthink.

dynamic dialogue cannot occur without diversity of opinion. Groups that cannot lean in the direction of different points of view fall quickly into groupthink. Their perceptions become rigid, and they can no longer see anything beyond the group's shared beliefs. Groupthink, a concept described by Irving L. Janis in "Groupthink: The Desperate Drive for Consensus at Any Cost," evolves when shared meaning goes bad. Instead of pursuing a common pool of meaning through rich and diverse conversation, the group finds one idea or belief and rigidly holds to it.

As members of a group fall deeper into groupthink, they view any "outside" ideas as a threat to their security and well-being. This can lead to a subtle form of group paranoia that leads the group to think it must protect itself from invaders who hold foreign ideas. Hmm... sounds a lot like certain pockets of evangelicalism.

Pliability counters groupthink because the group is not afraid to converse about topics that are outside its normal boundaries of discussion. Pliability enables a group to loosen its grip on ideas that could lead to unhealthy behaviors. Again, this is why diversity is such an important group quality. If everyone on your team thinks and acts as everyone else does, your team is susceptible to groupthink. Good leaders know this and so populate their teams with a variety of personalities and perspectives.

Pliability and Money

One topic of conversation that absolutely requires pliability is money. Leaders who cannot be challenged by members become rigid and willful in instilling their ideas about the church's money. Conversely, members who cannot bend toward leaders in conversations concerning money themselves become obstinate or obstacles to true dialogue.

My experience is that the frustration leaders and members cause each other concerning money is quite often more passive than aggressive. Usually leaders and members won't become outwardly belligerent toward each other, but they may become inwardly bitter and skeptical. I believe a lot of the messages I would hear if I could fulfill my fantasy would be riddled with bitterness or frustration. This is partially due to the lack of pliability in the conversation. Too many conversations about money (regardless of whether the leader or the member is doing the talking) are more a monologue than a dialogue.

Conversation Starters

- Do the leaders of your church exhibit rigid attitudes toward money? How about members of the congregation? Gently give examples, and encourage responses from the leaders and/or members present for this discussion. During this time, be sure to suspend judgment by cultivating pliability. Listen; don't react!

- Do members of your team or congregation have the opportunity to challenge assumptions and behavior concerning your church's budget? Or is the spending so controlled that there is no way to question it?

Are any areas constantly overlooked by those who make the decisions about money? Is it possible to challenge, in a positive way, the distribution of money throughout your church?

CHAPTER **9**

CONVERSING ABOUT METHOD:
Do You Notice the "How"
Behind the "What"?

AS A KID, I HATED PIANO LESSONS. I was in love with the idea of playing the piano. It was getting there that caused me so much pain. At some point in early elementary school, I began taking piano lessons. Ms. Davis, who was 157 years old when I met her, was my first piano teacher. Ms. Davis seemed to have just the opposite love than the one that captivated me. She seemed more interested in getting there than in the actual arrival. This caused immeasurable strife between us. She wanted me to practice every day; imagine that! Worse yet, she wanted me to practice pieces that I was certain would never "wow" a crowd—which, of course, is the whole point of playing the piano.

Early in my piano lessons, I was introduced to scales, arpeggios, and a number of method books. Method books contain variations on scales and arpeggios that develop dexterity and the overall deftness of the player. Actually, these method books are nothing more than instruments of torture inflicted by those who "can" on those who "can't." And I was certainly in the camp of the "can'ts." Ms. Davis, on the other hand, was in the camp of the "cans" and insisted that I spend time every day on method.

Playing these scales and other exercises created in me a hatred for the thing I thought I loved. Well, that's not exactly the right way to put it. These exercises put me in touch with something in my own character that seemed bent on disappointing Ms. Davis.

I quit piano a few years after beginning with Ms. Davis. In high school I flirted with the piano, and because I was a music major in college, I had to take at least two years of piano, which turned into four. Throughout my career as a piano player, I struggled with method. Oh, I grew up a little bit and endured it, but I never really understood what method was trying to show me. I do now.

First, working on method showed me something about myself. My distaste for and disinterest in method revealed that I didn't want to pay the price to become skilled. The pathway was laborious and boring. Surely there was an easier way! Second, working on method revealed something about the way I played the piano. When I did pay attention to method, it exposed mistakes or flaws in my execution. Noticing *how* I played enabled me to expand *what* I could play. Too bad it took me so long to figure this out.

Method was a mirror that showed me my blind and bright spots as a player and as a person. It also helped me cultivate an important quality: awareness. The real aim of method was to provide me *a way to pay attention to the way I played as I played*. Awareness of how you play while you play is one of the more important elements in playing the piano, not to mention in life itself.

Awareness and Learning in Your Actionspace

This last critical issue, method, is all about noticing how you do ministry as a team or a church during and after that ministry. The more you learn to notice the "how" behind the "what," the more the activity in your actionspace can morph to meet important needs. This awareness will reveal characteristics about your team and/or congregation; some qualities will need to grow, and others will need to go. This chapter, therefore, is not so much about one specific issue you face in your church as it is about a specific tool you can use to pay attention to all the ways the church expresses itself in its actionspace.

If there is one thing lacking in many churches, it is awareness about method and process. We simply do not watch ourselves doing ministry and learn from that observation. We are prone to just do the activity and move on to the next event. Yet noticing how we minister will reveal to a team or church the same two issues my piano method revealed to me.

> We simply do not watch ourselves doing ministry and learn from that observation.

First, it will reveal how our activity could change to increase its potency. Ministry, void of awareness, can easily become activity void of meaning or influence. Second, it will reveal character flaws that are thwarting effectiveness. Teams and congregations, void of awareness, can easily fall into a kind of rigidity that thwarts curiosity and learning.

As a team notices how it works, it becomes a group of learners. Much has been made in the last few decades of cultivating a learning organization. Chris Argyris, author of *On Organizational Learning*, pioneered the way for Peter Senge and others to write and teach about this concept. Even though these ideas are almost passé at this point, I believe few organizations—and fewer churches—have significantly integrated the concepts in their cultures.

One of the reasons I believe these concepts have not taken root is because of what it takes to become a community of learners. Consider how Peter Senge describes the demeanor of a learning leader:

> Few leaders understand the depth of commitment required to build a learning organization...it is disorienting and deeply humbling, because our old mental models were the keys to our confidence and competence. To be a real learner is to be ignorant and incompetent. Not many top executives are up for that.
>
> *"Learning Leaders," Executive Excellence, November 1999*

Conversation Starters

- Do you think your team pays attention to method and process?

- Do you have conversations about past ministry activity and events to evaluate and learn from those events?

- Do you believe the people on your team are learners? Give evidence for your answer.

- Is your team open to constructive criticism from people on and beyond the team? Give evidence for your answer.

- What do you think Senge means when he describes the learning leader as "ignorant"? Would you be comfortable with that title? What is at the heart of Senge's idea? How could you foster that kind of ignorance on your team?

- How would the complexion of your team change if you were all learners? How would it change if you paid attention to your method with the aim of learning and growing from the evaluation? How might that change your entire church?

There is a direct link between Senge's call for "ignorant" leaders and the cultivation of awareness. The power of paying attention to method is that it will reveal the areas in which you and your team or congregation are ignorant and in need of learning. There are few things as powerful as scales that show piano players that they are fooling themselves about their abilities. The same is true for a group. Paying attention to the "how" will reveal to you the blind spots that plague your team or thwart your entire church. But of course, this will require you to be curious and assume the posture of an ignorant learner. If you're up for it, the investment will pay off in that your team will thrive in chaos and find new ways to overcome tough situations with creativity and innovation. But it all begins with your group's ability to notice and evaluate itself with grace and its willingness to confront, as *Good to Great* author Jim Collins calls it, brutal reality.

EXPERIENCEercise

Set up a time to take your team to a ropes course. My friend and partner, Tim Edris, is one of the best adventure guides and experiential learning facilitators I know. He's led numerous groups through experiences that create team ambiguity and ignorance, which leads to new levels of learning and innovation. If you're interested in knowing more about experiential learning or taking your team through an experience, you can contact Tim at time@emergingleadersinstitute.org.

I have learned so much about teams and about myself by participating in Tim's experiences. I have also had the privilege of taking groups through these experiences with Tim. Each exercise is a method in and of itself that reveals teams' blind and bright spots. It's one of the best ways to become a learning leader and a learning team.

The Cycle of Learning: How to Pay Attention to Method

As I have worked with various teams over the years, I've noticed there is a definite cycle to paying attention to process and method. This three-part cycle enables a team to bring intentional energy and evaluation to its ministry activity and team dynamics. This cycle can work for a team that's in the middle of ministry

> Pausing reminds a team that it is finite and frail and in need of continuous learning.

activity and seeking to learn along the way, or it can serve as a template for a team to use in evaluating past ministry endeavors.

PAUSE

Teams that want to understand the "how" of their ministry activity must first pause long enough to give reflection a chance. A team must make space to engage in a conversation about method. And that space begins when the group decides to pause. Nothing can happen without it. Many teams and leaders avoid the pause because they believe it will take too much time away from "the important stuff," but this pause doesn't have to be long. They forget that, without reflection, the important stuff may lead to all kinds of problems. Further, a team that never pauses will end up believing it is invincible.

The pause allows the team to honestly examine and evaluate its ministry activity. The nonstop team uses activity as a way to avoid this examination and evaluation. The nonstop team is one step from becoming a nonlearning team. Pausing does more than initiate the cycle of awareness; it also reminds a team that it is finite and frail and in need of continuous learning.

The pastoral team at North Way has come to appreciate the pause in a very specific way. A few years ago, we decided we needed a regular time away to renew our commitment to

Conversation Starters }

- Does your team work nonstop, or does it know how to pause? Give evidence for your answer.

- If you're on a nonstop team, why does the team work this way? Is the team avoiding something?

- Brainstorm three ways your group could learn to pause. Be specific.

- Remember, the pause can occur during ministry activities, not just afterward. Pausing along the way gives a team the ability to "learn in motion"—adjusting and morphing along the way. Describe a time your team has paused along the way. What difference did it make to the process of doing ministry?

> Longer pauses have a way of changing the way we pause on a daily basis.

one another and to doing ministry together. This time away normally happens once a quarter and is led by a facilitator who is not part of our team. These pauses enable us to reflect more deeply on the "how" of our "what." They have become invaluable to us.

What I've noticed about these longer pauses is that they have a way of changing the way we pause on a daily basis. Although we have a long way to go, we are more willing to reflect on our ministry daily because of the influence of these regular times away. It's always difficult to balance pausing with the need to accomplish the work of the ministry. However, these times away are teaching our pastoral team to pause as we work long enough to redirect our attention to the things that matter most.

EXPERIENCEercise

Create a room or some kind of space in your offices where your staff is encouraged to pause for a moment of reflection during the day. A meditation room can be a very simple space with a candle and an open Bible. Encourage the staff to use the room to pause, even for a minute, for reflection and prayer. You will be amazed, over time, how this pause will change your staff's awareness of God, each other, and the work at hand.

EXPERIENCEercise

As a team, do something unrelated to the ministry. Go have fun. At the end of the fun, spend thirty minutes talking about the condition of your team. Discuss the biggest blind spot and brightest spot on your team. Discuss how you might make regular pauses habitual.

PROBE

Once a team creates the necessary space, it must probe into the "how" of method and look at it with a critical eye. Probing requires a combination of grit and grace. The team has to be willing to look at itself with a kind of ruthless honesty. Without this ruthless honesty, probing normally ends before it begins. Teams that don't have the courage to probe keep the conversation safe so that nothing penetrates the outer shell.

Conversation Starters }

- How would you rate your team's ability to reflect on the "how" of its ministry (poor, fair, good, great)? Explain your rating.

- Describe a time when probing and reflection led to better ministry. What can you learn about that time that could assist you in future reflections?

On the other hand, if a probing conversation is not conducted with grace, it ends up looking a whole lot like a session of blame and maybe even shame. Tenderness must exist alongside ruthlessness, or the probing will only hurt individuals on the team. Grit and grace—that's the ticket when it comes to probing.

Probing requires a team to ask difficult questions about process and method. Questions that challenge established ministries or ways of doing things can indeed be threatening to individuals on a team or to the entire team. Individuals, sensing the conversation is getting a bit too close to home, can move into the emotional manipulation I described earlier. Don't forget the virtues of honesty, equanimity, and pliability when probing your methods.

> Grit and grace—that's the ticket when it comes to probing.

PERSEVERE

I will speak more about perseverance in the "Endtroduction." Suffice to say that there will come a point in the evaluation of method when the group will face inner and outer resistance. Let's face it: This kind of awareness and evaluation is going to be difficult at times. All teams have ways of deflecting the difficult information that comes along with probing. It's easier to give up on the process than to follow it through. Teams must learn to persevere through the hard part of evaluation in order to land on the shores of learning and transformation.

Groups use all kinds of mechanisms to avoid perseverance in the conversation about method. Some groups talk around an issue but never land on anything that could lead to change. Other teams change strategies every other day. This appears to be "cutting edge," but it's really a clever way to avoid sticking with it. Some teams use humor, anger, or other emotions to focus on the "dramatic" instead of anything that could lead to true change.

What Is *Your* Method Telling *You* About *Your* Team's *or* Church's Character?

I mentioned earlier that piano method revealed flaws in my personal character. If your team or community pays attention to how it does ministry, it, too, can learn a tremendous amount about itself. From communication patterns, to how the team handles stress and uncertainty, to the way your team taps its creative potential—the process of cultivating awareness and then conversing about your discoveries makes all the difference in the world.

The Conversation Starters on page 135 will help your team discover who it is when it does ministry. However, the best evaluations will come as your team learns to reflect on what is happening as it happens.

Conversation Starters

- How does your team deflect threatening conversations about method and ministry activity? Do you talk around an issue without ever getting to it? Do you use change as a smoke screen? How about emotional drama? Is there another way you avoid probing method and process?

- Would you describe your team as one that follows through or one that flits? Give evidence for your answer.

What Is *Your* Team Showing *You* About How *You* Minister in *Your* Actionspace?

The second way awareness of method can assist your team or congregation is by revealing the quality of your ministry activity. How do you evaluate your ministry activity and determine if it should change? If we're not careful, ministry activity can fall prey to the modern method of assembly-line production. We just keep doing our little part on the assembly line. We never challenge or question the activity—we just do it. "Just doing it" has a numbing effect that makes it hard to ever change the activity or the team.

I've provided the Conversation Starters on page 136 to help you examine and evaluate your actionspace and ministry activity, but ultimately your team knows the best questions to ask about these issues. The way to discover the right questions is by cultivating awareness. Begin watching your team and its ministry activity. Watch what emerges and what messages are hidden in the activity. You'll be amazed by what you find.

Remember the change that occurred on my team when we discovered a new way of delivering spiritual formation resources to our community. All of that stemmed from of a willingness to pause, probe, and persevere. We had no idea what would emerge, but we knew that our faithfulness to the process would yield something of great value. The same can happen to your team.

Remember, doing ministry activity is not enough. The "how" of the process (method) reveals important characteristics about the team and the ministry activity itself. Pay attention!

Conversation Starters

- When your team executes ministry activity, is there a noticeable synergy?

- Do you find that your team easily loses focus when times get hard? If so, what quality do you believe is missing from your team in these moments?

- Is there hidden tension on your team that is sabotaging its ability to collaborate?

- If you had to describe your team's personality, what adjectives would you use and why?

- How does your team handle conflict, chaos, and uncertainty?

- How creative and innovative is your team? What would increase innovation on your team? What do you think blocks innovation?

- How would you describe your team's greatest character strength and its greatest flaw? Be specific, and give evidence for your answers.

Conversation Starters

- What ministry activities in your actionspace are most in line with your mission identity? Which activities are least in line with your mission identity? Spend some time evaluating both types of activity. Why do you continue to do both types of ministry activity? Why are you reluctant to let go of the activity that doesn't match your identity?

Evaluate a specific ministry activity in light of the following questions.

- Are you satisfied with how you do this ministry?

- Is there anything about the processes associated with this activity that could be changed to increase the activity's effectiveness?

- Is your team doing its best or just going through the motions as it implements this ministry? If it is just going through the motions, why is this the case? How could the team reconnect to the passion it once had for the ministry? Or is it possible that this lack of passion is telling you something about the team or the validity of the ministry? Is the team tired, or is the ministry activity tired?

- Has this ministry activity or the team lost connection with the mission of the church? Has this ministry activity or the team lost connection with its own vision? If so, what would it take to reconnect it?

- Is there anything about the way the members of the team work together that should change? Do people understand their roles? Do they know how to synergize their efforts for maximum effect? Do they feel valued?

ENDTRODUCTION:
Singing Your Way to Dynamic Dialogue

From the Gut

I WAS A VOICE MAJOR IN COLLEGE. Because of this, one of the very first things I learned to do was, well...breathe. You'd think after eighteen years of nonstop breathing, I would have known how to do it. Nope. It's a fairly common problem; young singers don't understand the mechanics of breathing. And, without a proper understanding, everything else from voice control to tone to power is affected.

A novice singer tends to breathe from the upper chest and thereby reduces his or her overall ability. My teachers taught me to expand my chest outward (intercostal breathing), and, more important, to breathe from my diaphragm. The diaphragm is located a half inch to an inch above your navel. It is the place from which you can take your deepest breaths and sustain your tone with the most control.

My teachers taught me that my lower abdomen muscles, below my navel, were also critical to good singing. These muscles provided further support that allowed me to sing with greater control and skill. I finally learned that breathing deeply from the diaphragm, while simultaneously squeezing the lower abdomen muscles, was a great foundation for singing. "It's a lot like throwing up," one of my teachers declared. And with that, I knew how to breathe. All I needed was a whole lot of practice.

When the novice doesn't breathe properly, all kinds of problems can spoil good vocal production. One of the most common is that the singer tends to sing from the throat. He or she squeezes and tightens the throat muscles in an attempt to produce a pleasing and powerful sound. It never works. And it leads to all kinds of vocal problems, such as strain and even something as bad as vocal nodes (a callus that develops on the vocal cords).

My teachers spent most of their time teaching me where to apply pressure (diaphragm and lower abdomen) and where to relax (my throat and vocal cords). This is the best way to sing, but it is not easy to learn. It felt more natural and was far more tempting to ignore my diaphragm and abdomen and sing from a tight and pinched throat. Over time, though, the body remembers what is rehearsed again and again, and I eventually got the process down, and it became second nature.

To me, dynamic dialogue is a lot like good vocal production. You need a strong foundation in order to support the process. But if you don't relax, your team or congregation will end up producing pinched tones and/or developing a strain that makes it difficult to converse over the long haul. As we end our journey together, let me suggest a way to keep the foundation of the conversation simultaneously strong and relaxed.

Commitment: The Strong Foundation

The foundation of dialogue is commitment. In the days ahead, as you and your team seek to converse dynamically, it will require you to remain firmly committed to one another and to the process. You must fight the temptation to go back to old ways of conversing that lead to control, manipulation, or monologue. It will take time to learn this art, so you must be committed to weathering the inevitable frustrations and setbacks. If you give up at the first sign of stress, you'll not only revert to the old ways, but you'll also convince yourselves that true dialogue is not achievable. That's a one-two punch that can forever keep you in superficial chatter.

> You must fight the temptation to go back to old ways of conversing that lead to control, manipulation, or monologue.

Your commitment to honor God's emerging work, the various and divergent viewpoints and personalities in the church, and the discovery of a common and shared meaning provide the foundation needed to keep the conversation and the QUEST alive. Don't give up. This book and the information in it can be consistently revisited and renewed. The commitment to do so is the foundation you'll need to sustain the conversation for the long haul.

Practice: Developing a Relaxed Conversational Posture

If commitment is the foundation of dynamic dialogue, practice is what creates a relaxed posture that ensures the conversation remains rich in tone and powerful in wisdom. The biggest mistake you and your team could make is to give these concepts "a try," then give up on them. When it comes to dialogue, practice makes for a settled and relaxed team that can navigate ambiguity with grace and celebrate discovery with gratitude.

> Practice makes for a settled and relaxed team that can navigate ambiguity with grace and celebrate discovery with gratitude.

Try to view dynamic dialogue as an art form. This will help you avoid the mentality that you can conquer or perfect the process. Instead, you will view yourself as growing in your accomplishment of the art form. The more you practice, the more you increase your ability. But you can never hit the ceiling of your ability. Just as a concert pianist can practice ten hours today and still find ways to improve tomorrow, so your team can always grow as conversational artists.

The more we practice an art form, the more relaxed we become during the act of creation. If your team practices only occasionally, it will be obvious when its members converse. You will find yourselves succumbing to monologues and pinched chitchat. But if you continue to practice, you will find that your conversations will begin to change into the kind of group artistry I've described in this book. Practice, practice, practice! Relax, relax, relax. The QUEST and conversation await you.

Conversation Starters }

- Which of the two essentials of dynamic dialogue—commitment and practice—is lacking on your team or in your church? What could you do to establish that essential? For that matter, what could you do to more firmly establish both essentials?

- Much of the cultivation of commitment and practice (and everything else in this book) comes down to an intentional choice. What specific choices can you make that will ensure that dynamic dialogue becomes a part of the culture of your team and congregation? Discuss ways to infuse the church with the principles in this book. Build in specific times and mechanisms to evaluate your progress. The more intention you bring, the more fruit you will see over time.

Does Your Church Offer Marriage Insurance?

Great marriages don't just happen—husbands and wives need to nurture them. They need to make their marriage relationship a priority.

That's where the HomeBuilders Couples Series® can help! The series consists of interactive 6- to 7-week small group studies that make it easy for couples to really open up with each other. The result is fun, non-threatening interactions that build stronger Christ-centered relationships between spouses—and with other couples!

Whether you've been married for years or are newly married, this series will help you and your spouse discover timeless principles from God's Word that you can apply to your marriage and make it the best it can be!

The HomeBuilders Leader Guide gives you all the information and encouragement you need to start and lead a dynamic HomeBuilders small group.

The HomeBuilders Couples Series includes these life-changing studies:
- Building Teamwork in Your Marriage
- Building Your Marriage (also available in Spanish!)
- Building Your Mate's Self-Esteem
- Growing Together in Christ
- Improving Communication in Your Marriage (also available in Spanish!)
- Making Your Remarriage Last
- Mastering Money in Your Marriage
- Overcoming Stress in Your Marriage
- Resolving Conflict in Your Marriage

And check out the HomeBuilders Parenting Series™!

- Building Character in Your Children
- Establishing Effective Discipline for Your Children
- Guiding Your Teenagers
- Helping Your Children Know God
- Improving Your Parenting
- Raising Children of Faith

Look for the **HomeBuilders Couples Series and HomeBuilders Parenting Series** at your favorite Christian supplier or write:

Bringing Timeless Principles Home

www.familylife.com

P.O. Box 485, Loveland, CO 80539-0485.
www.grouppublishing.com

Revolutionize Your Small Group!

Christian Living from A to Z: A Bible Study Project for Women's Groups

Sherri Harris

A is for ability. B is for blessing. C is for courage…and Z? Zeal! Scrapbooking takes on a new dimension when group members work on their individual scrapbooks depicting Christlike values. You'll share memories and discover Bible truths! The 26-week Bible study includes one-page devotions to paste in your scrapbook (on acid-free paper), stencils, ideas, and a leader guide. Build relationships, dig into the Word and discover the artist within you! Part of Group's Scripture Scrapbooks™ series.

ISBN 0-7644-2555-2

Fruit of the Spirit: A Bible Study Project for Women's Groups

Sherri Harris

Here's a fresh, hands-on approach to women's small group studies! This innovative study combines thought-provoking devotions on the Fruit of the Spirit with scrapbook activities that dramatically reveal the wondrous ways God is growing his children toward maturity. It's Bible study that's fun, fulfilling and faith-building! Covering love, joy, peace, patience, kindness, goodness, faithfulness and self-control, each lesson and activity fosters deeper relationships with God (and others in the group!) and inspires continual growth.

ISBN 0-7644-2645-1

Sherri Harris lives in Fort Collins, Colorado, with her husband Steve. They have been married 30 years and have raised three children. Sherri and Steve have been in full-time ministry for 25 years, the past eleven serving at Timberline Church. Sherri ministers with her husband in the areas of worship and marriage ministries. The couple team-teach at marriage enrichment retreats. Sherri also has been a Bible study teacher, a retreat speaker, MOPS mentor, and workshop teacher.

Learn It, Live It Bible Studies™ Series

Fruit of the Spirit, Prayer, Spiritual Disciplines, Spiritual Gifts

It's the way Bible study should be! These small group studies have participants studying a topic, then choosing an engaging project to do as a group, reinforcing what they just learned. Includes several project options for each study, from easy one-night projects to more involved ideas.

Each title includes one leader guide and 6 participant books:

Fruit of the Spirit	**ISBN 0-7644-2556-0**
Prayer	**ISBN 0-7644-2557-9**
Spiritual Disciplines	**ISBN 0-7644-2558-7**
Spiritual Gifts	**ISBN 0-7644-2559-5**

CounterCultural Christians: Exploring a Christian Worldview With Charles Colson

Are you ready to develop a Christian worldview—then transform culture? Gain deep insights in a fun-to-learn format with this interactive media kit! Video and audio presentations from Charles Colson set the stage for each session's dynamic group discussions. Participants will grasp the underlying belief systems that impact how people view the world around them—then dig into Scripture for guided conclusions. This easy-to-lead course is great for Sunday school or small groups.

CounterCultural Christians multimedia kit comes with materials to make an impact:

- 12 flexible sessions fuel well-balanced Christian perspectives on current events
- Video with twelve 3- to 5-minute segments featuring Charles Colson
- CD with 12 *BreakPoint* audio segments
- Leader Guide with tips and background information for each session
- 6 Participant Guides with relational questions and activities

ISBN 0-7644-2520-X

Go Deeper with Chuck Colson

Playing God?:
Facing the Everyday Ethical Dilemmas of Biotechnology

Hosted by Charles Colson
and Nigel M. de S. Cameron,
Ph.D. Tracey D. Lawrence

This dynamic multimedia study brings Charles Colson, one of the foremost voices in America on the topic of integrating faith and life, and Nigel M. de S. Cameron, Ph.D., a highly respected bioethics expert, to your class or group. In this easy-to-learn format, they introduce bioethical topics and the Christian faith, and talk about how a worldview applies to these topics. The two dispel myths with solid, accurate information. And participants are motivated to talk about cloning, in vitro fertilization, stem-cell research, euthanasia, the future, and more! Heavy topics—deep on insight—are sure to get everyone involved, thinking, and realizing they understand these hot issues a little bit differently than before. Participants will discover how bioethical topics are relevant to them, and they'll have a better appreciation for God's precious creation—life!

Playing God? includes:

1 Leader Guide—Easy-to-follow tips will help any leader direct interactive, thought-provoking sessions.

1 Video—Features Colson or Cameron introducing each session with a 3- to 5-minute overview. It'll launch exciting discoveries! Some clips include interviews with scientists or topical experts.

1 CD—Each session features a related Charles Colson commentary from his nationally syndicated daily radio program, BreakPoint.

1 BreakPoint Transcripts Booklet—Perfect for helping leaders better prepare lessons! There is a transcript for each of the broadcasts on the CD.

6 Participant Guides—Each participant will need a copy to answer questions and make personal life applications.

Flexible and easy to use, *Playing God?* is great for small-group use, Sunday school/Bible study classes, college ministry, or as a teaching series.

ISBN 0-7644-2642-7

Charles Colson is a popular author, speaker, and radio commentator. Founder of the international ministry Prison Fellowship and host of the nationally syndicated BreakPoint radio program, he is one of the foremost voices in America on the subject of integrating faith and life. Colson and Tracey D. Lawrence also collaborated on *CounterCultural Christians: Exploring a Christian Worldview.*

Nigel M. de S. Cameron, Ph.D. is dean of The Wilberforce Forum and is an educator, author, editor, and a recognized authority in bioethics. He served as advisor on the US delegation to the UN special meeting on human cloning and is a frequent guest on TV shows such as *Nightline* and *Frontline.*

Tracey D. Lawrence is a freelance writer and founder of *Scribe Ink.* She holds a B.S. in Christian Education and an M.A. in Church History and Theology. Lawrence has worked with such ministries as The Wilberforce Forum, Promise Keepers, Christian History Institute, and Focus on the Family.

EVALUATION FOR

Discovering Your Church's Future
Through Dynamic Dialogue

Please help Group Publishing, Inc., continue to provide innovative and useful resources for ministry. Please take a moment to fill out this evaluation and mail or fax it to us. Thanks!

Group Publishing, Inc.
Attention: Product Development
P.O. Box 481
Loveland, CO 80539
Fax: (970) 292-4370

● ● ●

1. As a whole, this book has been (circle one)
   not very helpful   *very helpful*
   1   2   3   4   5   6   7   8   9   10

2. The best things about this book:

3. Ways this book could be improved:

4. Things I will change because of this book:

5. Other books I'd like to see Group publish in the future:

6. Would you be interested in field-testing future Group products and giving us your feedback? If so, please fill in the information below:

Name_____

Church Name   _____

Denomination _____ Church Size _____

Church Address   _____

City _____ State_____ ZIP _____

Church Phone _____

E-mail   _____